JOURNEY
Mark Link, S.J.

**A meditation program
based on**
The Spiritual Exercises of St. Ignatius

Valencia, California   Allen, Texas

Imprimi Potest
   Robert A. Wild, S.J.

Unless otherwise noted, Scripture passages are taken from
The New American Bible with Revised New Testament
© 1970, 1986 by the Confraternity of Christian Doctrine,
Washington, D.C. All rights reserved.

Photo Credits

David Daniel   92
Mark Link, S.J.   vi, 12, 22, 42, 52, 62, 72, 82, 102
Mike Powell/All Sport, Inc.   Front cover
Peter Simon/Peter Arnold, Inc.   32

Send all inquiries to:
Tabor Publishing
25115 Avenue Stanford, Suite 130
Valencia, California 91355

Printed in the United States of America

ISBN 0-89505-654-2 (*Challenge*)
ISBN 0-89505-655-0 (*Decision*)
ISBN 0-89505-656-9 (*Journey*)

1 2 3 4 5   92 91 90 89 88

CONTENTS

Author's Preface

Physical exercises—swimming, climbing, hiking—are ways to improve circulation, breathing, and muscle tone. In short, they are ways to improve physical fitness and bodily health.

"Spiritual exercises"—meditation, contemplation, vocal prayer—are ways to do the same for the human spirit. In short, they are ways to improve spiritual fitness and spiritual health.

Journey is the final phase of a three-phase meditation program called The Challenge Program. The first phase is found in a book called *Challenge;* the second phase, in a book called *Decision.* The Challenge Program is based on *The Spiritual Exercises of St. Ignatius.* For a brief description of Saint Ignatius' Exercises, see Appendix A in the back of this book.

There are three ways you can use *Journey.* An ideal way is with the help of a spiritual guide and as part of a support group (eight to ten people) that meets weekly with the guide. The guide's role is discussed in Appendix B. The format for the group meetings is discussed in Appendix C.

A second way to use *Journey* is alone, under the direction of a spiritual guide.

A final way is by yourself, without a guide or a support group. This is not the best way, but it may be the only way possible for you. If you follow this option, try to consult occasionally with a spiritual guide.

Lent 1988   Mark Link, S.J.

1
OPPOSITION

Can you face rejection as Jesus did?

They picked up stones to throw at Jesus.
John 8:59

Two music critics covered a concert by a Russian pianist in New York City years ago.

The critic for the *New York Times* summed up the concert, saying, "It was a disappointing evening. One had hoped for more technical and musical refinement. Because of constant experimentation with the tempos, the work sounded disconnected."

The critic for the New York *Herald Tribune* summed up the same concert in these words: "Two-thousand-candlepower playing by the Soviet Thor of the piano . . . electrified to cheers an audience which uses its hands more often to stifle yawns than to applaud the musicians."

These two contradictory reviews of the same performance recall a line from Oscar Wilde's *Reading Gaol:* "Two men looked out through prison bars—one saw mud, the other stars."

1

What was true of the two music critics and the two prisoners was also true of people's response to Jesus. Some saw his miracles and heard his teaching and said, "This is truly the savior of the world." *John 4:42* Others heard and saw the same things and said, "He is out of his mind. . . . He is possessed by Beelzebul." *Mark 3:21-22*

Just as people in biblical times rejected Jesus, so people today reject his followers. Jesus warned this would be so, saying, "If the world hates you, realize that it hated me first. . . . No slave is greater than his master." *John 15:18, 20*

This week's meditations focus on the rejection Jesus received and the rejection you can expect if you try to follow Jesus closely. So the grace you ask for is this:

Lord, help me face rejection
as courageously as you did.

The following passages describe people's rejection of Jesus.

Jesus and Beelzebul	Luke 11:14-23
Words of eternal life	John 6:53-71
The man born blind	John 9:1-41
The plot	John 11:45-57
The world's hatred	John 15:18-25

The meditations and readings for this week set the stage for the events of Holy Week, the ultimate opposition and rejection of Jesus by his enemies.

As you begin the third and final phase of this meditation program based on *The Spiritual Exercises of St. Ignatius,* it may be well to review the procedure for meditating on each exercise. It involves three steps:

1. *Preparation*—setting the stage for meditation
2. *Presence*—creating the climate for meditation
3. *Prayer*—meditating

Step one: Preparation

Begin by recalling the grace you seek through your meditation. This grace differs each week and is specified in the introduction to the week.

Next, read the Scripture passage that gives the theme of the daily meditation. After reading it, pause briefly to review it in your mind and to let it sink into your heart.

Next, read the story that develops the theme of the daily meditation. Again, pause briefly to review it in your mind and to let it sink into your heart.

Lastly, *reread* the Scripture passage slowly and prayerfully. It is God's Word.

Step two: Presence

This step consists in putting yourself in God's presence. One way to do this is to close your eyes, relax your body, and monitor your breathing.

As you focus on your breathing, recall that breath points to God's presence within you. The Book of Genesis says, "The LORD God . . . formed a man . . . he breathed life-giving breath into his nostrils and the man began to live." *Genesis 2:7 (TEV)*

Breathing also points to the presence of the Holy Spirit within you. Jesus said to his disciples, " 'Peace be with you. As the Father sent me, so I send you.' Then he breathed on them and said, 'Receive the Holy Spirit.' " *John 20:21-22 (TEV)*

If God makes his presence felt (for example, if you feel deep inner tranquility and peace), do not move on. Simply remain in a posture of openness and silent communication with God as long as it lasts— even if it is for the entire meditation period. Trying to *make* yourself feel God's presence, however, is almost always wrong. Feeling God's presence is a gift. If God wishes to give it to you, that is up to God. Your role is to keep your mind and heart open to God's will.

Step three: Prayer

Once you have placed yourself in God's presence, begin your reflection on the Scripture passage and the meditation story. To facilitate your reflection, a brief meditation guide has been placed at the end of each story. The purpose of this guide is not to restrict your meditation, but to stimulate it. Use the guide or not, as you see fit.

Conclude your meditation by doing two things: (1) reread the Scripture passage prayerfully, and (2) speak to God from your heart, as the Spirit moves you.

One final point. Continue to write down your insights, resolutions, and feelings in the space following each meditation. A few brief sentences will do. From time to time you might want to review your journal entries. Many people find such reviews to be occasions for gratitude and insight.

You are now ready to begin the final phase of your meditation program. Begin with the confidence that God wishes to bless you in a special way in the days ahead.

Day one

*A division occurred in the crowd
because of Jesus.
Some of them even wanted to arrest him.*
John 7:43–44

The Battle of Gettysburg left fifty thousand soldiers dead or wounded. Months later, on November 19, 1863, President Lincoln delivered a brief dedication address at the military cemetery at Gettysburg.

The Harrisburg *Patriot and Union* said of the address, "We pass over the silly remarks of the President. . . . We are willing that the veil of oblivion shall be dropped over them and they shall no more be repeated."

The Chicago *Times* said of the address, "The cheek of every American must tingle with shame as he reads the silly, flat, and dish-watery utterances of . . . the President of the United States."

Today, all agree that the Gettysburg Address is one of the greatest utterances of American history.

In a similar way, the words of Jesus were ridiculed by many of the people of his time. But today, even nonbelievers admit that "never before has anyone spoken" as Jesus did. *John 7:46* Nor has anyone since spoken as Jesus did.

How much does fear of rejection or ridicule keep you from doing and saying what you think is right? *Speak to Jesus about how he handled this fear.*

_____
_____
_____
_____
_____
_____

*The Son of Man must suffer greatly
and be rejected.*   Mark 8:31

The two Cleveland teenagers who created Superman were told repeatedly by comic-strip editors that their idea was "stupid" and "unbelievable." The youths eventually sold all rights to the cartoon for $130.

In the early days of his career, superstar Bill Russell was criticized for his defensive style in basketball. Bill says in *Sports Illustrated:*

Before I came along there were virtually no blocked shots in the game of basketball. . . . As late as my sophomore year in college, my coach was telling me that my defensive style was "fundamentally unsound."

Many of Jesus' teachings ("love your enemies") were also considered "stupid" or "fundamentally unsound" by people in his time. Many people still don't take them seriously.

Thomas Carlyle was probably close to the truth when he said, "If Jesus were to come today, people would not crucify him. They would ask him to dinner, hear what he had to say, and make fun of him."

How seriously do you take *all* the teachings of Jesus? *Speak to Jesus about your fidelity to hard teachings, like "love your enemies" and "pray for those who mistreat you."*   Luke 6:27-28

Day three

Jesus' family . . .
set out to take charge of him,
because people were saying, "He's gone mad!"
Mark 3:21 (TEV)

In 1842, Congress didn't take Samuel Morse seriously when he explained to them his plans for a national telegraph system. Senator Smith of Indiana thought Morse might be mentally ill.

In 1876, the president of Western Union laughed at Alexander Graham Bell, calling the telephone he invented a useless "toy."

In 1878, the British Parliament ridiculed Thomas Edison's plans for an electric light, calling his invention "unworthy of the attention" of the scientific community.

In 1908, people scoffed at Billy Durant for suggesting that cars would someday replace the horse and buggy.

In 1921, Tris Speaker criticized Babe Ruth, saying, "Ruth made a big mistake when he gave up pitching" and became an outfielder.

In 1940, military experts scorned the suggestion that the helicopter had military value.

When was the last time you encouraged or praised someone? Criticized or put someone down? *Speak to Jesus about how he was able to cultivate and maintain a positive approach toward people and life.*

Day four

"Can anything good come from Nazareth?"
John 1:46

One day a partially deaf boy came home from school with a note from his teacher. He handed it to his mother.

She opened it slowly and read it. As she did, she choked back tears. The note suggested that her son was too dull to learn. He was holding back the whole class. It would be better for everybody if he would withdraw from school.

When the boy's mother finished reading the note, she felt awful. She also felt challenged. "My son, Tom, is not too dull to learn," she said to herself. "I'll teach him myself."

When Tom died many years later, the entire nation honored him in a remarkable way. At exactly 9:59 P.M., Eastern Standard Time, every home in the United States turned off its lights for one minute, as a tribute to the man who had invented those lights.

Thomas Edison invented not only the electric light but also the movie projector and the record player. When he died, the boy who was "too dull to learn" had over a thousand patents to his credit.

How much do you let other people's negative remarks or judgments discourage you? Recall an example. *Speak to Jesus about how he handled discouragement and depression.*

_____

_____

_____

_____

_____

_____

Day five

Jesus said, "Father, forgive them,
they know not what they do." Luke 23:34

Everyone has heard of Bugs Bunny, but practically no one has heard of Charles Jones. Yet it was Jones who developed the Bugs Bunny cartoon.

Jones's favorite cartoon character, however, wasn't Bugs Bunny. It was Pepe LePew, the romantic skunk. Pepe was forever falling in love with someone. His love was always rejected, however, because of the odor he gave off.

But that didn't stop the indomitable Pepe. He just kept right on loving—and right on being rejected. That's what made everyone, eventually, love Pepe. He never gave up on people or on love.

Although Charles Jones never intended the connection, Pepe makes a beautiful image of Jesus. Jesus never gave up on people or on love either. He went right on loving, no matter how many times he was rejected.

How do you respond when people reject your attempts to love or reach out to them? *Speak to Jesus about his refusal to give up on people, even though they rejected his love and concern.*

9

He came to what was his own,
but his own people did not accept him.   John 1:11

One night a fisherman heard a loud splash. A man on a nearby yacht had been drinking and had fallen overboard. The fisherman leaped into the cold water, rescued the man, and revived him with artificial respiration. Then he put the man to bed, and did everything he could to make him comfortable. Finally, exhausted by the ordeal, the fisherman swam back to his own boat.

The next morning the fisherman returned to the yacht to see how the man was doing. "It's none of your business," the man shouted defensively. The fisherman reminded the man that he had risked his life to save him. But instead of thanking him, the man cursed the fisherman and told him that he never wanted to see him around again. Commenting on the episode, the fisherman said:

I rowed away from the yacht with tears in my eyes. But the experience was worth it, because it gave me an understanding of how Jesus felt when he was rejected by those he saved.

Relive the fisherman's experience of being cursed and told to leave. *Speak to Jesus about the need to refuse to give up on people like the yachtsman.*

_____
_____
_____
_____
_____
_____

Day seven

They picked up stones to throw at Jesus.   John 8:59

If you can trust yourself when all men doubt you,
But make allowance for their doubting too . . .
Or being lied about, don't deal in lies,
Or being hated, don't give way to hating,
And yet don't look too good, nor talk too wise;

If you can dream—and not make dreams your master;
If you can think—and not make thoughts your aim;
If you can meet with triumph and disaster
And treat those two imposters just the same;
If you can bear to hear the truth you've spoken
Twisted by knaves to make a trap for fools,
Or watch the things you gave your life to broken,
And stoop and build 'em up with wornout tools;

If you can walk with crowds and keep your virtue,
Or walk with kings—nor lose the common touch;
If neither foes nor loving friends can hurt you,
If all men count with you, but none too much;
If you can fill the unforgiving minute
With sixty seconds' worth of distance run,
Yours is the Earth and everything that's in it,
And—which is more—you'll be a Man, my son!

Rudyard Kipling, "If"

Reread the poem, pausing after each stanza to reflect on how it applied to Jesus as opposition against him mounted and spread. *Speak to Jesus about this.*

_____

_____

_____

_____

_____

2
LORD'S SUPPER

Do you understand the Eucharist?

> *"I am the living bread*
> *that came down from heaven;*
> *whoever eats this bread will live forever."*   John 6:51

An artist designed an unusual door for a church in Cologne, Germany. He divided it into four panels, each depicting a symbol that referred to a gospel event.

The first panel depicts six water jugs, symbols of the miracle of Cana, where Jesus changed water into wine.

The second panel depicts five loaves and two fish, symbols of the miracle near Capernaum, where Jesus multiplied bread and fish to feed a hungry crowd.

The third panel shows thirteen people around a table, symbolizing the Last Supper, where Jesus broke bread and said, "Take it; this is my body."   *Mark 14:22*

The fourth panel shows three people around a table, symbolizing the Emmaus supper on Easter Sunday night.

The artist's door is an excellent biblical summary of the Lord's Supper, or Eucharist. It traces the Eucharist from Cana, where it was prefigured, to Capernaum, where it was promised, to Jerusalem, where it was instituted, to Emmaus, where it was celebrated for the first time on Easter Sunday night.

The meditations for this week focus on the Lord's Supper. The grace you ask for is this:

Lord, deepen my understanding of the Eucharist, which I celebrate weekly at your table.

During the week you may wish to read about the gospel events that the German artist referred to in the panels of his church door.

The Eucharist prefigured	John 2:1–11
The Eucharist promised	Luke 9:10–17, John 6:51–56
The Eucharist instituted	Mark 14:1–26
The Eucharist celebrated	Luke 24:13–35

During the week you may also wish to celebrate the Eucharist on one or several mornings in your parish church. This is merely a suggestion. The important thing is to be attentive to anything the Holy Spirit may move you to do.

Day one

"Do this in memory of me." Luke 22:19

A man made a dramatic turnaround in his life. When asked how he did it, he pulled out a snapshot from his wallet. It was a picture of a caseworker who had helped him years before.

"Whenever I feel tempted to fall back into my old ways," the man said, "I *remember* what this caseworker did for me, and I draw strength from his *memory.*"

That story illustrates an important biblical truth. For ancient Jews, *remembering* a religious event meant far more than calling to mind something that happened centuries before. On the contrary, *remembering* the event meant bringing it into the present and reliving it by faith.

Thus when Jews *remembered* the Passover each year, they did far more than call to mind the event that freed their ancestors from Egypt. Rather, by remembering, they brought that event into the present and relived it again. In this way, they received the same blessing from it that their ancestors did.

It was with this understanding that Jesus and his disciples gathered to celebrate the Passover meal on Holy Thursday night.

Recall the memories of some persons or events that still give you joy and strength. *Speak to God about one of these memories.*

15

Day two

*Jesus poured water into a basin
and began to wash the disciples' feet.*   John 13:5

Jews normally ate two meals daily: one around ten in the morning, the other, later in the afternoon. The Passover meal, however, was eaten at night, just after the first stars appeared. Thus everyone celebrated it at the same time as one family.

As Jesus and his disciples waited for the first stars, they could see Passover fires blazing throughout Jerusalem.

When the stars appeared, Jesus, acting as the father, began the Passover ceremonies. Strangely enough, he did so by removing his outer robe and washing the feet of his disciples. For Jews, washing another's feet was humiliating. Only slaves washed people's feet. Thus Jesus' action created a deep impression on his disciples. He said to them:

"What I am doing, you do not understand now, but you will understand later. . . . I have given you a model to follow, so that as I have done for you, you should also do. . . . If you understand this, blessed are you if you do it."   John 13:7, 15, 17

Recall a time when you "washed another's feet" (performed a humble service for another without being asked). Imagine Jesus washing your feet right now. *Speak to Jesus about the feelings this sets up in you.*

_____

_____

_____

_____

_____

_____

Day three

"One of you will betray me." Mark 14:18

After Jesus had explained to his disciples why he had washed their feet, he took wine and passed it around, saying, "Take this and share it among yourselves." *Luke 22:17* Drinking from the same cup dramatized the unity of the diners. Red wine was usually drunk at Passover meals to recall the blood-marked doorposts in Egypt and the covenant blood at Mount Sinai.

Jewish meals normally began with "breaking of bread." The Passover meal, however, began with the eating of bitter herbs. This afforded the cue for the youngest to ask, "Why is tonight's meal different?"

The father then explained the meaning of the foods eaten at the Passover meal. The bitter herbs "remembered" the years of bitter slavery in Egypt. The unleavened bread "remembered" the hasty departure from Egypt; the Israelites did not even wait for the next day's bread to rise. The lamb "remembered" the Lord's command to mark each Hebrew house with blood to spare it from the tenth plague.

During the sharing of the bitter herbs, Jesus said to his disciples, " 'Amen, I say to you, one of you will betray me, one who is eating with me.' They began to be distressed and to say to him, one by one, 'Surely it is not I?' "

Recall a time when you betrayed Jesus (sinned). *Speak to Jesus about it and ask his forgiveness.*

17

"This is my body,
which will be given for you." Luke 22:19

The eating of the bitter herbs was followed by the traditional "breaking of bread." A reverent silence fell upon the disciples as Jesus picked up the loaf of bread with his weather-beatened hands.

Then he took the bread, said the blessing, broke it, and gave it to them, saying, "This is my body, which will be given for you; do this in memory of me."

                                                            Luke 22:19

The disciples were struck by Jesus' reference to his body. Perhaps some of them recalled that day in the synagogue in Capernaum, when Jesus said, "I am the living bread that came down from heaven; whoever eats this bread will live forever; and the bread that I will give is my flesh for the life of the world." *John 6:51*

As the disciples ate it they undoubtedly sensed that something marvelous was taking place.

_____

Imagine you are present at the table as Jesus says, "This is my body, which will be given for you." Study the eyes of Jesus as he says this. Study the other disciples as they look at Jesus and ponder his words. *Speak to God about the feelings welling up in your heart.*

_____
_____
_____
_____
_____
_____

Day five

"This is my blood."   Mark 14:24

After everyone had eaten, Jesus poured the cup of wine that concluded the Passover meal. Again, a reverent silence fell over the disciples as Jesus took the cup into his hands and said, "This cup is the new covenant in my blood, which will be shed for you." *Luke 22:20*

The disciples were struck by Jesus' reference to a "new covenant." It recalled God's promise to Jeremiah: "Days are coming . . . when I will make a new covenant with the house of Israel and the house of Judah." *Jeremiah 31:31*

The disciples were also struck by Jesus' reference to "blood" being poured out for them. It recalled the old covenant, when Moses poured blood on the people, saying, "This is the blood of the covenant which the LORD has made with you." *Exodus 24:8*

As the disciples passed the cup from one to the other, their minds were filled with questions. Had they just witnessed the fulfillment of God's promise of a "new covenant"? What did Jesus mean when he said his own blood would be shed for them?

What motivates you to gather each Lord's Day at the Lord's table to eat the Lord's Supper? What motivates you to continue to gather, when others have ceased to gather regularly? *Speak to Jesus about this.*

_____

_____

_____

_____

_____

_____

Day six

I shall not die, but live.   Psalm 118:17

The disciples' minds were reeling as Jesus ended the Passover meal by singing the traditional Hallel. No doubt tears flooded their eyes as they joined Jesus in singing the song that Jews had been singing now for a thousand years.

> *The cup of salvation I will take up,*
> *and I will call upon the name of the LORD. . . .*
> *Precious in the eyes of the LORD*
> *is the death of his faithful ones. . . .*
>
> *I shall not die, but live,*
> *and declare the works of the LORD. . . .*
> *The stone which the builders rejected*
> *has become the cornerstone. . . .*
>
> *This is the day the LORD has made;*
> *let us be glad and rejoice in it. . . .*
> *Give thanks to the LORD, for he is good;*
> *for his kindness endures forever.*
> Psalm 116:13, 15; 118:17, 22, 24, 29

What song holds emotional memories for you? Reread the words of the Hallel, pausing after each stanza to reflect on how it applied to Jesus as he began his final twenty-four hours on earth. *Speak to Jesus as the Spirit moves you.*

_____

_____

_____

_____

_____

Day seven

*As often as you eat this bread
and drink the cup,
you proclaim the death of the Lord
until he comes.*   1 Corinthians 11:26

Mark ends his description of the Last Supper, saying, "After singing a hymn, they went out to the Mount of Olives." *Mark 14:26*

The disciples were happy as they walked along under the stars. But it was a bittersweet happiness. Jesus had said too many sorrow-shadowed things. His final words, especially, kept ringing in their ears: "Do this in memory of me."

Years after the Last Supper, Paul wrote to Christians in Greece, "As often as you eat this bread and drink the cup, you proclaim the death of the Lord until he comes."

Paul's point is important. Jesus is present in a mysterious way in every celebration of the Eucharist, or Lord's Supper. But the *fullness* of his presence will be realized only when he returns in glory.

Until then, the Lord's Supper will always be a paradox of presence and absence. It will be a call "to mourning as well as to feasting, to sadness as well as to joy, to longing as well as to satisfaction."

Henri Nouwen

What part of the celebration of the Lord's Supper is most meaningful to you? Least? Why? *Speak to Jesus about this.*

21

3
LORD'S SUPPER TODAY

How much do you appreciate the Eucharist?

The bread that we break,
is it not a participation
in the body of Christ?   1 Corinthians 10:16

Prior to Vatican II, Catholics did not eat or drink anything for twenty-four hours before receiving Communion. During this era Father Walter Ciszek was arrested by the Russians and accused of being a "Vatican spy." He spent the next twenty-three years in prisons and labor camps. When released, he wrote a book about his experiences. In one passage he describes how prisoners celebrated the Lord's Supper. They would rise early and eat it in secret, knowing they would be severely punished if caught. This made it hard for many prisoners to participate. Father Ciszek writes in *He Leadeth Me:*

We would consecrate extra bread and distribute Communion to the other prisoners when we could. Sometimes that meant we would only see them when we returned to the barracks at night for dinner. Yet these men would actually fast all day long and do exhausting physical labor without a bite to eat since the evening before, just to be able to receive the Holy Eucharist—that was how much the sacrament meant to them.

This week's meditations focus on a personal appreciation of the Lord's Supper. The grace you ask for is this:

Lord, deepen my love for the Lord's Supper,
which I celebrate weekly at your table.

During the week you may wish to celebrate the Eucharist on one or several mornings in your parish church or elsewhere. This is merely a suggestion. The important thing is to be attentive to whatever the Holy Spirit moves you to do.

Finally, you might wish to read and meditate on these two brief but beautiful passages concerning the Eucharist in Paul's First Letter to the Corinthians.

One loaf, one body   1 Corinthians 10:16–17
"In memory of me"   1 Corinthians 11:23–34

Day one

"Do this in memory of me."   Luke 22:19

Each year Catholics celebrate the feast of Corpus Christi ("Body of Christ"). The purpose is to honor the eucharistic Body of Christ by carrying it in procession as a sign of gratitude to the Lord for this great gift. Why set aside a special day for this? Isn't the Body of Christ honored in each celebration of the Lord's Supper? We set aside a special day for this feast for the same reason that we set aside Thanksgiving Day. We do it because of our human tendency to take God's gifts to us for granted.

Here is how an African bishop describes a two-mile-long Corpus Christi procession in Nigeria in 1986, which was held in spite of a downpour of rain.

The people danced and sang in the rain. It was the first time I recall the Blessed Sacrament being carried . . . to the sound of . . . cheering and clapping. Everyone was drenched. No one thought of seeking shelter or running away. Judges, lawyers, doctors, mothers, children stood their ground as if nothing was happening except the Eucharist. I have not seen anything like it here or anywhere else.   America magazine

Recall a celebration of the Lord's Supper or Corpus Christi that was especially meaningful to you. How deep is your appreciation of God's gift of the Eucharist? *Speak to God about this.*

_____

_____

_____

_____

_____

_____

25

Day two

We, though many, are one body,
for we all partake of the one loaf.   1 Corinthians 10:17

Astronauts Aldrin and Armstrong landed on the moon July 20, 1969. While Armstrong prepared for his moon walk, Aldrin unpacked bread and wine and put them on the abort guidance system computer. He describes what he did next:

I poured the wine into the chalice. . . . In the one-sixth gravity of the moon the wine curled slowly and gracefully up the side of the cup. It was interesting to think that the very first liquid ever poured on the moon and the very first food eaten there were communion elements.   Guideposts Treasury of Hope

Just before eating and drinking the elements, Aldrin read this passage from the Gospel according to John: "I am the vine, you are the branches. Whoever remains in me and I in him will bear much fruit, because without me you can do nothing."
John 15:5

Commenting on his Communion experience on the moon, Aldrin says, "I sensed especially strong my unity with our church back home, and the Church everywhere."

———————

What kind of unity do you feel with your home church? With the Church everywhere? *Speak to Jesus about these feelings—or lack of them.*

_____

_____

_____

_____

_____

_____

Day three

"My Lord and my God!" John 20:28

Steve Garwood is a South Carolina building contractor. The first Sunday after his child was born, he brought the Body of Christ home to his wife. She was still recuperating. When he opened the door, he saw that some friends had dropped in to see the new baby. So he placed the pyx containing the Body of Christ on an icon shelf in the living room.

Visitors streamed in all day. By the time the last one left, Steve had not yet had time to be alone with his wife, who had just fallen asleep.

As he passed through the darkened living room on his way to bed, Steve felt compelled to kneel in reverence before the Body of Christ in the pyx. As he knelt there, with bowed head, it suddenly struck him that he was not alone in the room. The Lord was with him. This sudden realization totally overwhelmed him. He wrote later:

Blood pounded in my ears and all the hairs of my body stood on end. I thrust my face to the floor and spread my hands out in supplication before me. "Lord Jesus Christ, Son of God," I said, "have mercy on me, an ungrateful sinner. You are here before me, in my house, and you have blessed me so much."

And You, Who Do You Say I Am?

Recall the most meaningful experience you ever had before the Blessed Sacrament in a church. *Speak to Jesus about why he chose to make himself present to us in this sacramental way.*

Day four

*"Where two or three
are gathered together in my name,
there am I in the midst of them."* Matthew 18:20

A religious persecution in 1980 left a region of Guatemala without priests. But the people continued to meet in the various parishes.

Once a month they sent a delegate to a part of Guatemala where priests still functioned. Traveling up to eighteen hours on foot, the delegate celebrated the Lord's Supper in the name of the parish. Describing one of these celebrations, Fernando Bermudez writes in his book *Death and Resurrection in Guatemala:*

The altar was covered with baskets of bread. After the Mass, each participant came up to take his or her basket home again. Now the bread was Holy Communion for the brothers and sisters of each community.

In time the authorities closed all the churches. But the people refused to stop gathering, recalling Jesus' words, "Where two or three are gathered together in my name, there am I in the midst of them." They said to themselves, "If the authorities forbid us to meet in the churches, we shall gather under the trees of the wood or in the caves of the mountains."

Why do you gather each Lord's Day around the Lord's table to eat the Lord's Supper with the Lord's people? *Speak to Jesus about his decision to make himself present in a special way at this time.*

Day five

*You are Christ's body,
and individually parts of it.* 1 Corinthians 12:27

William Barclay tells the story of an old African chief of the Ngoni tribe. One Sunday morning he sat at the Eucharist, watching members of the Ngoni, Senga, and Tumbuka tribes worshiping side by side. Suddenly his mind flashed back to his boyhood, and he recalled watching Ngoni warriors, after a day's fighting, washing Senga and Tumbuka blood from their spears and bodies.

That morning at the Eucharist, the old chief understood as never before what Christianity is all about. It is God, calling all people in and through Christ to put away all hostility and live as one family.

This is the earthshaking message that Jesus entrusted us to preach to all nations. It is a message that cannot be spoken by a single person. It must be spoken by the whole Christian community in every nation on earth. For here on earth, we are Christ's body; we are Christ's voice. If we are silent, Christ is silent. If one of us is silent, a part of Christ is silent. If a part of Christ is silent, a part of his message goes unheard.

———————————

Do you think of yourself as being a part of Christ? Do you think of your silence about Christ's message as silencing a part of Christ? *Speak to Jesus about the responsibility Christians have to the world.*

Jesus Christ is our peace.   Ephesians 2:14

Some members of the French underground were arrested by the German army and sentenced to death by firing squad. On the eve of their execution, the prisoners, mostly Catholic, asked to celebrate the Lord's Supper. The German guard explained that the only priest available was German. After discussing the matter, the prisoners agreed to accept the priest. They concluded that it was not his nationality or his politics that were at issue, but his role as a Catholic minister.

Now, one of the German guards at the jail happened to be Catholic also. Even though he might be picked to be part of the firing squad in the morning, he asked to join the French prisoners at Mass.

In such a situation one might question whether it was possible for the prisoners to allow the guard to share the Lord's Supper with them. How could they permit someone to share their meal of Christian unity if he might end up being their executioner? After discussing the matter, a spokesperson told the guard, "Leave your rifle outside the door if you wish to join us."

Imagine you are one of the French prisoners celebrating the Lord's Supper. What would be your thoughts as you turned to the German guard to give him a handshake of peace? *Speak to Jesus about this.*

Day seven

*Jesus came and stood in their midst
and said to them, "Peace be with you."*   John 20:19

The "eye" of a hurricane is a remarkable thing. To get an idea of what it is like, picture a Frisbee with a small hole cut out of its center. Expand the Frisbee so that it measures a hundred miles across and the small hole measures ten miles across. Next, spin the Frisbee at the rate of one hundred miles per hour. That's what a hurricane is like. But keep in mind that inside the ten-mile "eye" of the hurricane there is no wind—only blue skies and a shining sun.

The hurricane's "eye" is an image of what the Eucharist is intended to be. Political storms may rage about us, but in the Eucharist there is a peaceful calm, blue skies of hope, and a shining "Son" of love.

Just as the "eye" of a hurricane lasts only about an hour as it passes over, so the Eucharist lasts only an hour.

But Jesus never intended that we stay in the "eye" of the Eucharist. He intended that we go back into the storm and become an "eye" of peace to others. He intended that we share with others the Prince of Peace, which we have received in our hearts.

Recall the most meaningful eucharistic celebration you ever experienced. What made it special? *Speak to Jesus about how the Eucharist can become more meaningful in your life.*

31

4
AGONY IN THE GARDEN

Can you say, "Your will be done"?

"Father, all things are possible to you.
Take this cup away from me,
but not what I will but what you will." Mark 14:36

There was no radar to guide artillery shells in World War I. Missiles were simply lobbed over hills and trees much as one lobs a rock over a brick wall at some hidden target.

To remedy this situation, artillery officers used to go aloft in hot-air balloons to locate the target and give directions to their gunners. They would yell down, "A little to the left" or "A little to the right."

Going up in the balloon was a dangerous job, because the person in the balloon was a perfect target for enemy gunfire. One artillery officer said that just the thought of going up in the balloon made him "sweat blood."

We can all relate to how that officer felt. We too have had to do things we dreaded doing.

Jesus was no exception. He also had to do things he dreaded doing. One of them was facing the ordeal that lay ahead of him on Good Friday.

This week's meditations focus on Jesus' agony in the Garden of Gethsemane, when Jesus actually "sweat blood" thinking about what the next day would bring (Luke 22:44). The grace you ask for is this:

Lord, help me face life's trials
with the same courageous acceptance
that you demonstrated in the garden.

As you read the gospel account of Jesus' agony in the exercises for this week, keep in mind what Atticus Finch told his children in the novel *To Kill a Mockingbird*. He said that the only way to understand people is to crawl inside their skins and walk around with them.

This is also true of understanding the Gospel. You can never understand the Gospel by "reading" it. You must "contemplate" it. That is, you must crawl inside the skin of its characters and walk around with them. Therefore, if you are to understand the agony in the garden, you must crawl inside the skin of Jesus and experience in your imagination what he experienced.

You are now ready to "contemplate" the passion (suffering) of Jesus. As you begin, keep in mind that "contemplating" this portion of the Gospel has changed more people's lives and made more saints than any other portion of the Gospel.

Day one

"My soul is sorrowful even to death."
Matthew 26:38

After the Last Supper, Jesus and his disciples went to the Garden of Gethsemane on the Mount of Olives. Jesus took Peter, James, and John with him and disappeared into the darkness.

Jesus said to them, "My soul is sorrowful even to death. Remain here and keep watch with me." He advanced a little and fell prostrate in prayer, saying, "My Father, if it is possible, let this cup pass from me; yet, not as I will, but as you will."

When he returned to his disciples he found them asleep. He said to Peter, "So you could not keep watch with me one hour? Watch and pray that you may not undergo the test. The spirit is willing, but the flesh is weak." Withdrawing a second time, he prayed again, "My Father, if it is not possible that this cup pass without my drinking it, your will be done!" Then he returned once more and found them asleep. . . . He left them and withdrew again and prayed a third time, saying the same thing again.

Then he returned to his disciples and said to them . . . "Behold, the hour is at hand. . . . Look, my betrayer is at hand." Matthew 26:38–46

Climb inside Jesus' skin and experience everything he did in the garden. Why ask God for something if you are going to end up saying, "Not as I will, but as you will"? *Speak to Jesus about this.*

Day two

"Your will be done!"   Matthew 26:42

Robert Granat's short story "The Sign" concerns a young man named Davidson. He wants to be a writer and has just mailed his first novel to a publishing house. Filled with fear about the publisher's decision, he goes outside and paces back and forth in an orchard. It was Holy Week.

His thoughts went back and forth between Christ and himself, like a needle and thread: to Christ in the garden of Gethsemane, kneeling in prayer, and to himself in the orchard . . . to Christ preparing for the supreme agony of hanging by nails . . . back to himself and his book with Dow Press. . . . He stopped and said . . . "Thy will, not mine."

But then "a bolt of awareness" struck him. He *really* didn't mean what he said. What he *really* meant was that he wanted God's will to be done "if it coincided with his own will and worked out 'right,' to the joint glory of the pair of them, God and Davidson. And for the moment he was nauseated." Then he sat down and cried.

Recall a time when you wanted something badly and you prayed to God for it. Did you add, "Your will be done"? *Talk to Jesus about "his will" for your life.*

Day three

Jesus prayed again,
"My Father . . . your will be done!"   Matthew 26:42

Catherine Marshall was the wife of Peter Marshall, the famous chaplain of the United States Congress. At one period in her life she became critically ill. No amount of medicine and prayer seemed to help.

One day she read about a missionary who had been sick for eight years. The missionary prayed unceasingly for health. Finally, she resigned herself to God's will, saying, "Lord, I give up. If you want me to be an invalid, fine." Within weeks, the missionary experienced a remarkable recovery.

Catherine thought the story strange. But she could not dispel it from her thoughts. Finally, she too resigned herself to God's will, saying, "I'm tired of asking. You decide what you want for me." And what was the result? Catherine describes it this way in *Guideposts:*

It was as if I had touched a button . . . as if some dynamo of heavenly power began flowing. . . . Within a few weeks I had experienced the presence of the living Christ in a way that wiped out all doubt. . . . From that moment my recovery began.

Do you ever say, "Lord, help me to know and do your will. What is it that you want me to do?" *Speak to Jesus about the difficulty of doing this.*

Day four

Jesus said to them, "I AM." John 18:5

Jesus was talking with his disciples when Judas entered the garden with a crowd. Judas went over to Jesus and kissed him. Greeting a friend with a kiss was common among oriental males. It was also the prearranged sign by which Judas agreed to identify Jesus for the soldiers. Jesus turned to them and said:

"Whom are you looking for?" They answered him, "Jesus the Nazorean." He said to them, "I AM." . . . When he said to them, "I AM," they turned away and fell to the ground. So he again asked them, "Whom are you looking for?" They said, "Jesus the Nazorean." Jesus answered, "I told you that I AM. So if you are looking for me, let these men go." . . . So the band of soldiers, the tribune, and the Jewish guards seized Jesus and bound him. John 18:4–8, 12

The Greek word for "I am he" may also be translated "I AM." It is the same word the Old Testament uses to refer to God (Yahweh). The context shows that John intends his use of the word in this instance to be translated "I AM," for at its sound the soldiers "fell to the ground."

Climb into the skin of the arresting soldiers and experience what they did when Jesus said, "I AM." Feel what Judas felt then. *Speak to Jesus about why he spoke those words at that moment.*

_____
_____
_____
_____
_____
_____

Day five

They turned away and fell to the ground.   John 18:6

When Jesus identified himself with the words "I AM," the soldiers "fell to the ground." Ancient writers tell us that two great Roman leaders, Mark Antony and Marius, had a similar impact on their assassins.

The sound of their voices was sufficient to strike terror into the men sent to murder them, but the latter were only individual assassins in circumstances quite different.

It may very well be that in this instance, the guards suddenly felt the full force of Jesus' personality and were utterly dismayed. . . . In any case it is obvious . . . that John intends to picture it as miraculous, thereby emphasizing the perfect freedom with which Jesus accepted arrest.   Giuseppe Ricciotti

There Jesus stood, completely alone and unarmed. There the soldiers stood, a hundred strong and completely armed. Yet it was the soldiers, not Jesus, who fell back in fear. There flowed from Jesus something that, in all his aloneness, made him mightier than all his enemies.

Imagine what it was like to stand in the presence of Jesus. Recall a time when you sensed a great inner power radiating from a person. *Speak to Jesus about what radiated from him.*

_____

_____

_____

_____

_____

_____

Day six

"If you are looking for me,
let these men go." John 18:8

Ernie Pyle was a newspaper columnist who lived in the trenches with the soldiers in World War II. He jotted down in a notebook what he heard them say. For example, one young man said, "I'm fighting hard, Mr. Pyle, but it's hell out here. At times, when the big guns get whaling away, when snipers start poppin' from the hedges, I just want to fold my tent."

Ernie Pyle also jotted down what he saw. In one of his columns he wrote:

Take a West Virginia boy I saw yesterday. . . . He always carries a little chunk of coal in his pocket. He's a miner, from a family that's always mined, and when he gets battle depression he reaches into his pocket and clenches that bit of coal. Then he says to himself, "If I can take the mines, I can take this."

Although something divine radiated from Jesus, he had only a human body and a human heart, as we have. He experienced the same terrifying fear and bitter depression that we sometimes experience. Yet, in Gethsemane, in the face of overwhelming fear and depression, Jesus exercised uncommon courage.

———————

Recall a time when you were filled with fear or depression. How did you surmount it? *Speak to Jesus about the fear and depression he felt in Gethsemane—and how he overcame it.*

————————————————————————

————————————————————————

————————————————————————

————————————————————————

————————————————————————

Day seven

*"Shall I not drink the cup
that the Father gave me?"*   John 18:11

A fitting signature to Jesus' agony in the garden
is the peace he exhibited after it was all over.

Although his disciples had deserted him and he
stood alone before his enemies, Jesus stood there with
a composure that made him mightier than they.
William Barclay draws this comparison between the
Jesus who entered the garden and the Jesus who left
it. He writes:

*A famous pianist said of Chopin's nocturne in
C-sharp minor, "I must tell you about it. . . . In this
piece all is sorrow and trouble . . . until he begins to speak
to God, to pray; then it is all right."*

Barclay then draws his comparison:

*That is the way it was with Jesus. He went into
Gethsemane in the dark; he came out in the light—
because he talked with God. He went into Gethsemane
in agony; he came out with peace in his soul—because
he talked with God.*

Recall a time when you entered into prayer
deeply disturbed and came out of prayer deeply
composed. *Talk to Jesus about prayer's healing power.*

41

5
WAY OF THE CROSS

Why did Jesus suffer for you?

They continued their shouting,
"Crucify him! Crucify him!" Luke 23:21

Albrecht Durer was a famous sixteenth-century German painter. One of his masterpieces is called *Descent from the Cross.*

A moving detail in the painting shows one of the disciples holding the crown of thorns that was removed from Jesus' head. He is pressing his finger against one of the thorns to learn how much pain Jesus felt when the crown was pressed into his flesh.

This week's meditations focus on the suffering of Jesus, which began after his arrest and lasted until his death. The grace you ask for is this:

Lord, teach me how much you suffered for me,
that I may know how much you love me.

During the week you may feel moved to pray the Stations of the Cross. This is a devotion in which you accompany Jesus, in spirit, on his journey to Golgotha. If you can't make the stations in a church, you may make them at home. The procedure for making them is simple. Just pause briefly at each station, imagining you are there in person. Hear what Jesus heard; see what Jesus saw; try to feel what Jesus felt. End each meditation by speaking to Jesus in your own words. Here is a list of the fourteen stations:

1. Jesus is condemned to death.
2. Jesus carries his cross.
3. Jesus falls the first time.
4. Jesus meets his mother.
5. Jesus is helped by Simon.
6. Jesus' face is wiped by Veronica.
7. Jesus falls a second time.
8. Jesus speaks to the women.
9. Jesus falls a third time.
10. Jesus is stripped of his clothes.
11. Jesus is nailed to the cross.
12. Jesus dies.
13. Jesus is taken down from the cross.
14. Jesus is laid in the tomb.

Day one

Peter began to curse and to swear,
"I do not know the man."
And immediately a cock crowed.
Then Peter remembered the word
that Jesus had spoken:
"Before the cock crows
you will deny me three times."
He went out and began to weep bitterly.
Matthew 26:74–75

Jesus was taken in chains from Gethsemane to the high priest's house. Shortly after they arrived, Peter showed up in the courtyard. Someone saw him and accused him of being Jesus' disciple. Overcome with panic, Peter swore that he never knew Jesus.

Peter's panic-stricken action recalls a scene from the novel *Lord Jim*. Jim went to sea as a boy and spent hours at the ship's rail, dreaming of doing brave things at sea. Eventually he grew up and became the skipper of the *Patna*. One night the *Patna* struck something and began to sink. In a fit of unexplainable panic, Jim leaped into the sea to save himself. With that leap went all his boyhood dreams. Although braver hands saved the ship and its eight hundred passengers, Jim never forgave himself.

Years later Jim bought back his salvation. He gave his life in a splendid act of courage that exceeded his wildest boyhood dreams. With that act he was able to forgive himself—and was forgiven.

Recall a mistake you made and had a hard time forgiving yourself for. *Speak to Jesus about it.*

"Tell us," they said,
"are you the Messiah? . . .
Are you . . . the Son of God?"
Jesus answered them, "You say that I am."
And they said, "We don't need any witnesses!
We ourselves have heard what he said!"
Luke 22:67, 70–71 (TEV)

The next morning the guards took Jesus before the Jewish Council. Numbering seventy people, it was a kind of Jewish Supreme Court, with its own police and its own power of arrest. Council members sat in a half circle. The prisoner stood in the center, facing them. When the verdicts were given, each member, starting with the youngest, faced the prisoner and passed judgment.

When the Council had completed its essential interrogation of Jesus, it came directly to the point and asked him:

"Are you the Messiah? . . . Are you . . . the Son of God?" Jesus answered them, "You say that I am." And they said, "We don't need any witnesses! We ourselves have heard what he said!"

Jesus' response was interpreted as blasphemy and, therefore, deserving of death (Matthew 26:66). But lacking the power to pass the death sentence, the Council took Jesus to Pilate to ask for it.

What assures you most that Jesus was telling the truth in his response? *Speak to Jesus about it.*

Day three

"Crucify him! Crucify him!" Luke 23:21

A boy was picked to represent his class in a play about Jesus' crucifixion. An internationally famous troupe had asked local people to make up the crowd scene. For a week the boy looked forward to his glamorous appearance on stage with real actors.

An hour before curtain time, the people in the crowd scene were gathered together and given their instructions. The director pointed to twelve men in red turbans and said, "There are your leaders. Do exactly as they do and shout exactly what they shout."

Minutes later the boy found himself on stage. On a balcony stood Jesus. Next to him stood Pilate. The boy describes what happened next:

"Give us Barabbas," the crowd shouted. I joined in, screaming with them. "What shall I do then," boomed the voice from the balcony, "with Jesus who is called the Christ?" "Crucify him!" the roar went up. I yelled those terrible words. I know I did. I heard myself shouting!

Suddenly I was cold. I was shaking uncontrollably. . . . I don't know when I started to cry, but tears were streaming down my face and I was moaning, "No, no, no!" Drew Duke, *Guideposts*

Relive the small boy's experience. *Speak to Jesus about it and how it applies to your life.*

_____

_____

_____

_____

_____

Day four

Then Pilate took Jesus and had him scourged.
John 19:1

During Holy Week of 1986, *USA Today* carried a front-page story about the crucifixion of Jesus. It was based on an article by a doctor in the *New England Journal of Medicine.*

The doctor said Christians tend to romanticize the death of Jesus. In reality, it was the most brutal death you could imagine.

Ancient writers tell us that scourgings or floggings often preceded crucifixion. It was not uncommon for victims to die before the flogging was over. Ancient writers also tell us that victims of crucifixion sometimes went insane. They spent their final hours on earth completely out of their mind.

One ancient writer reports that after the fall of Jerusalem in A.D. 70, Jewish freedom fighters waged guerrilla warfare against the Romans. One day the leader of a guerrilla group was captured. The Romans threatened to crucify him in plain sight of the others, who were firmly entrenched in caves on a steep hillside. The rest of the guerrillas surrendered rather than see their leader suffer such a humiliating and horrible execution.

What is the worst physical pain you ever suffered? The worst mental pain? *Speak to Jesus about the worst pain he suffered during his crucifixion.*

Day five

Then they spat in Jesus' face and struck him,
while some slapped him, saying,
"Prophesy for us, Messiah;
who is it that struck you?"   Matthew 26:67-68

"Parker's Back" is a short story by Flannery O'Connor. It's about a man named Parker, who lives with his wife, Sarah Ruth, in a poor shack in the deep South.

Sarah Ruth constantly badgers Parker about his lack of religion. She also despises the tattoos that cover his body. Determined to please her, just once, Parker decides to go out and have a tattoo of Jesus needled on his back.

When Parker returns, he shows the tattoo to his wife. She snarls like an enraged dog and screams, "Idolatry!" Then she grabs a blunt instrument and beats him savagely across the back. Parker is too stunned to resist. Flannery O'Connor concludes her story, saying of Parker:

He sat there and let her beat him, until she nearly knocked him senseless and large welts had formed on the face of the tattooed Christ. Then he staggered up and made for the door.

Recall a time when you inflicted physical or mental abuse on someone. *Speak to Jesus about why people hurt each other this way.*

Day six

*The soldiers wove a crown out of thorns
and placed it on Jesus' head.*   John 19:2

In his book *Deliver Us from Evil,* Dr. Tom Dooley tells about treating an old priest who was punished by the Communists in southeast Asia for "preaching treason." His punishment was a mock crown of thorns. Eight nails were driven into his head: three in the front, two in the back, and three across the top. Dooley writes:

I washed the scalp, dislodged the clots, and opened the pockets to let the pus escape. I gave the priest massive doses of penicillin and tetanous oxide. . . . The old man pulled through.

That story bears out the words of Michael Quoist in his book *Prayers of Life:*

The Way of the Cross winds through our towns and cities, our hospitals and factories, and through our battlefields; it takes the road of poverty and suffering in every form. It is in front of these new Stations of the Cross that we must stop and meditate and pray to the suffering Christ for strength to love him enough to act.

Where do you see Jesus suffering in the city or neighborhood? *Ask Jesus for the wisdom to know what to do about this and for the strength to do it.*

*Pilate . . . handed Jesus over
to be crucified.*   Mark 15:15

Father Titus Brandsma was a university president in Holland during World War II. He was arrested by the Nazis and taken to a concentration camp at Dachau.

There he was isolated in an old dog kennel. His guards amused themselves by ordering him to bark like a dog when they passed. Eventually the priest died from torture. What the Nazis didn't know was that he had kept a diary of his ordeal, writing between the lines of print in an old prayerbook. On one page we find this poem to Jesus:

*No grief shall fall my way, but I
Shall see your grief-filled eyes;
The lonely way that you once walked
Has made me sorrow-wise. . . .*

*Your love has turned to brightest light
This night-like way [of mine]. . . .*

*Stay with me, Jesus, only stay;
I shall not fear
If, reaching out my hand,
I feel you [are near].*

Could you endure such an ordeal? Reread the poem slowly and prayerfully. *Pause after each stanza to speak to Jesus about how it applies to your life.*

6
CRUCIFIXION

Why did Jesus die for you?

They came to the place called the Skull.   Luke 23:33

The science-fiction story "The Traveler" is about a scientist named Paul Jairus. He's part of a research team that has invented an energy screen that makes it possible to travel backward into time.

Jairus is picked to make the first flight. He decides to fly back to the crucifixion of Jesus. Jairus is a nonbeliever and anticipates finding it quite different from the way the Bible describes it.

Soon Jairus finds himself soaring backward into history—one hundred years, one thousand years, two thousand years. Minutes later the energy screen touches down on target. The crucifixion site is swarming with people.

Jairus asks the Command Center to allow him to move closer to the crosses. They grant it, but warn him to stay inside the energy screen.

Jairus moves in. As he does, his eyes come to rest on Jesus. Suddenly something unexpected happens. He feels drawn to Jesus like a tiny piece of metal is drawn to a magnet. He is deeply moved by the love radiating from Jesus. It's something he never experienced before.

Then, contrary to all his expectations, the events of the crucifixion unfold exactly as the Gospel describes them. Jairus is visibly shaken.

The Command Center realizes this and fears he is becoming emotionally involved. They tell him to prepare for immediate return to the twentieth century. Jairus protests, but to no avail.

The return trip goes smoothly. When Jairus steps from the energy screen, he is a changed man.

This week's meditations focus on the crucifixion of Jesus. The grace you ask for is this:

Lord, help me contemplate your death
in a way that I may be changed by it.

As you meditate on the crucifixion this week, you may want to keep a crucifix or a picture of the crucifixion before you. If you use a crucifix, you may wish to end each meditation by kissing the five wounds of Jesus: his pierced hands, his pierced feet, and his pierced side.

You may also feel moved to want to pray the five sorrowful mysteries of the rosary. They are:

1. Jesus agonizes in the garden.
2. Jesus is scourged.
3. Jesus is crowned with thorns.
4. Jesus carries his cross.
5. Jesus dies on the cross.

Again, these are merely suggestions. The important thing is to open yourself in a loving, trusting way to whatever the Holy Spirit may inspire you to do.

Day one

The people stood by and watched;
the rulers, meanwhile, sneered at Jesus
and said,
"He saved others, let him save himself
if he is the chosen one, the Messiah of God."
Luke 23:35

There comes a time when we must face life alone. There comes a time when the sky turns dark and we are all alone. There comes a time when we feel totally abandoned, even by God. That time came for Jesus on the cross. Mark describes it this way:

At noon darkness came over the whole land until three in the afternoon. And at three o'clock Jesus cried out in a loud voice, "Eloi, Eloi, lema sabachthani?" which is translated, "My God, my God, why have you forsaken me?" . . . Jesus gave a loud cry and breathed his last. . . . When the centurion who stood facing him saw how he breathed his last he said, "Truly this man was the Son of God!" . . .

When Pilate learned of Jesus' death from the centurion, he gave the body to Joseph. Having bought a linen cloth, he took him down, wrapped him in the linen cloth and laid him in a tomb that had been hewn out of the rock. Then he rolled a stone against the entrance of the tomb. Mark 15:33–39, 45–46

Recall a time when you felt totally alone, seemingly abandoned—even by God. *Speak to Jesus about his own feeling of abandonment on the cross.*

Day two

He humbled himself . . .
even death on a cross.
Because of this, God greatly exalted him . . .
Jesus Christ is Lord,
to the glory of God the Father. Philippians 2:8–9, 11

The curtain falls on the crucifixion with all eyes fixed on Jesus. Nothing matters but that solitary figure suspended between heaven and earth.

Two thousand years later, all eyes are still fixed on the man on the cross. An old man who survived the Nazi holocaust summed up the feeling of millions when he said:

As I looked at the man upon the cross . . . I knew I must make up my mind once and for all, and either take a stand beside him and share in his undefeated faith in God . . . or else fall finally into a bottomless pit of bitterness, hatred, and unutterable despair.
quoted by S. Paul Shilling

An American writer expressed his thoughts about the man on the cross this way:

Love may suffer but it overcomes. The man of faith has found in Jesus a hope stronger than history and a love mightier than death. Anthony Padovano

---

What attracts you most to the man on the cross? *Speak to Jesus about what he did, and why he did it that way.*

_____

_____

_____

_____

_____

_____

Pilate . . . had an inscription written
and put on the cross. It read,
"Jesus the Nazorean,
the King of the Jews." . . .
The chief priests of the Jews said to Pilate,
"Do not write 'The King of the Jews,'
but that he said,
'I am the King of the Jews.' "
Pilate answered, "What I have written,
I have written."   John 19:19, 21

Some years ago, divers located a four-hundred-year-old ship off the coast of northern Ireland. Among the treasures found on the sunken ship was a man's wedding ring. When it was cleaned up, the divers noticed that it had an inscription on it. Etched on the wide band was a hand holding a heart. Under the etching was this inscription: "I have nothing more to give you."

Of all the treasures on that ship, none moved the divers more than that ring and the beautiful inscription on it.

The words on that ring, "I have nothing more to give you," could have been written on the cross of Jesus. For on the cross, Jesus gave us everything he had. He gave us his love. He gave us his life. He gave us all that one person could give to another. He had nothing more to give us.

What are you prepared to give Jesus in return for all that he has given you? *Speak to Jesus about this.*

Day four

Christ Jesus . . .
gave himself as ransom for all.   1 Timothy 2:5–6

In April 1865, the slain body of President Lincoln lay in state for a few hours in Cleveland, Ohio. It was on its way from Washington, D.C., to Springfield, Illinois, where it would be buried.

In the long line of people filing by the body was a poor black woman and her little son. When the two reached the president's body, the woman lifted up her son and said in a hushed voice, "Honey, take a long, long look. That man died for you."

What that black mother said to her child can be said about Jesus by every mother to every child.

Real-life savior-heroes, like Jesus and Lincoln, stand in sharp contrast to TV savior-heroes, like nurses, teachers, and law-enforcement officers. They too save people: the brutalized child, the runaway teenager, the exploited senior citizen. But more often than not, they do so without great personal cost.

Real-life savior-heroes, like Jesus and Lincoln, tell a different story. They tell us that waging war against evil involves great personal cost and suffering— even the loss of one's own life.

What are some wrongs in today's world that you would be willing to suffer for to change and correct? *Speak to Jesus about what you might do.*

Day five

" 'Speak, LORD,
for your servant is listening.' " 1 Samuel 3:9

William Blatty, author of *The Exorcist,* has written another novel called *Legion.*

In one scene in *Legion,* Lieutenant Kinderman, a Jewish detective, is standing alone in Holy Trinity Church in Washington, D.C. A priest had just been brutally murdered while hearing confessions.

Kinderman looks down at the blood on the floor. It has trickled from under the confessional door into the aisle of the church. He sits down in a pew and shakes his head. Then he slowly lifts his eyes to a huge crucifix on the wall. As he gazes at it his face softens and a quiet wonder comes to his eyes. He begins to speak to Jesus on the cross:

"Who are you? God's son? No, you know I don't believe that. I just asked to be polite. . . . I don't know who you are, but you are Someone. Who could miss it? . . . Do you know how I know? From what you said. When I read, 'Love your enemy,' I tingle. . . . No one on earth could ever say what you said. No one could even make it up. Who could imagine it? . . . Who are you? What is it that you want from us?"

How would you answer Lieutenant Kinderman's last two questions? *Speak to Jesus about the answers he would give to the detective. About the answers he would give to you.*

59

Day six

*"No one has greater love than this,
to lay down one's life for one's friends."* John 15:13

The death of Jesus on the cross is a sign, an invitation, and a revelation.

First, it's a sign. It is a sign of the depth of Jesus' love for us. The crucifixion says in the most dramatic way possible what Jesus told his disciples so often in his lifetime: "No one has greater love than this, to lay down one's life for one's friends." *John 15:13*

Second, the death of Jesus is an invitation. The crucifixion invites us to love one another as Jesus loves us. It says in the most dramatic way possible what Jesus told his disciples so often in his lifetime: "Love one another as I love you." *John 15:12*

Finally, the death of Jesus is a revelation. It reveals to us something about love that we are prone to forget. The crucifixion says in the most dramatic way possible what Jesus told his disciples so often in his lifetime—that love entails suffering: "Whoever wishes to come after me must deny himself, take up his cross, and follow me." *Mark 8:34*

Recall the first time you learned firsthand that love entails suffering. Recall the most recent time you suffered for love. *Speak to Jesus about why he suffered for* you *in such a dramatic way.*

_____

_____

_____

_____

_____

_____

Day seven

Jesus Christ is Lord. Philippians 2:11

It was drizzling as a man walked alone one night across the wooded grounds of a retreat house. Suddenly he came upon a life-size crucifix. It was beautifully illuminated by a spotlight.

As the man drew closer, he saw trickles of water streaming down the face and body of Jesus. Tears came to the man's eyes. He thought of a card in his wallet, given to him by his wife years ago. It read:

> *I carry a cross in my pocket,*
> *A simple reminder to me. . . .*
> *This little cross is not magic*
> *Nor is it a good luck charm. . . .*
> *It's not for identification*
> *For all the world to see.*
> *It's simply an understanding*
> *Between my Savior and me. . . .*
> *It reminds me to be thankful*
> *For my blessings day by day*
> *And strive to serve him better*
> *In all that I do and say. . . .*
> *Reminding no one but me*
> *That Jesus Christ is Lord of my life*
> *If only I'll let him be.* Anonymous

Do you carry anything on your person that identifies you as a follower of Jesus? How clear is it from your behavior that you follow him? *Speak to Jesus about why it is hard to let him be Lord of your life.*

7
RESURRECTION

What happened Easter morning?

When the sun had risen . . .
they came to the tomb.
They were saying to one another,
"Who will roll back the stone for us
from the entrance to the tomb?"
When they looked up, they saw
that the stone had been rolled back. . . .
On entering the tomb they saw a young man
sitting on the right side,
clothed in a white robe,
and they were utterly amazed!
He said to them, "Do not be amazed!
You seek Jesus of Nazareth, the crucified.
He has been raised; he is not here."   Mark 16:2-6

An Associated Press reporter might have described the Good Friday events this way:

JERUSALEM (AP)—*Jesus of Nazareth was executed today outside the city walls of this ancient city. Death came at about three o'clock. A freak thunderstorm scattered the crowd of curious onlookers and served as a fitting climax to the brief but stormy career of the controversial preacher from the hill country of Galilee. Burial took place immediately. A police guard was posted at the grave site as a precautionary measure. The Galilean is survived by his mother.*

The events of Good Friday left the followers of Jesus in a state of shock. Their dream that he had been sent by God to bring about a better world ended in a grotesque nightmare. It was over. It was finished. It was ended.

But, in a matter of days, another incredible event took place. The disheartened followers of Jesus were amazingly transformed. Radiantly alive with new vision and power, they proclaimed the unbelievable message that Jesus had cheated death. He was risen.

No amount of persecution would stop them from preaching this "good news."

With the passage of time, some of Jesus' disciples were crucified for proclaiming this message. Others were ripped apart by wild beasts in the Roman Colosseum. Still others were burned alive at the stake. But nothing could stop them from preaching the "good news."

How can you explain the incredible turn of events that took place within days of Jesus' death? The only acceptable explanation is the one the disciples themselves gave: They had seen Jesus alive!

This week's meditations focus on the resurrection of Jesus. The grace you ask for is this:

Lord, help me grasp the reality
and the meaning of your resurrection.

Day one

When they entered,
they did not find the body of the Lord Jesus.
Luke 24:3

An old movie called *The World in Darkness* concerned an archaeological dig in Jerusalem. The site was the area where Jesus was buried. One day the archaeologist in charge announced that he had found the tomb of Jesus. Then came the bombshell! The tomb was not empty! There was a mummified corpse in it that fit the description of Jesus perfectly.

People came in huge crowds to look at it. Jesus had not been raised from the dead after all. The news media immediately flashed the story to the four corners of the earth. The Christian world was thunderstruck. The resurrection of Jesus had never taken place. It was all a hoax.

In anger, churches were closed or demolished. Crosses and Bibles were desecrated and destroyed. The Christian world was plunged into darkness.

Then, years later, on his deathbed, the archaeologist confessed that he had contrived the whole thing. The hoax was on his part.

Whatever the merit of the film, it has this value. It makes us realize that nothing is more important than a knowledge of what happened in Jerusalem on the first Sunday after the crucifixion of Jesus.

What is one way your life would be totally different today if Jesus had not risen? *Speak to Jesus about the most meaningful contribution his resurrection has made to your life.*

> *The apostles thought*
> *that what the women said was nonsense.*
> Luke 24:11 (TEV)

The Apostles' first reaction to the news that Jesus had arisen was disbelief. But soon Jesus began to appear to other disciples. For example, on Easter Sunday night, two disciples were returning to Emmaus, discussing the tragic weekend as they walked along.

Suddenly a stranger (Jesus) joined them, and they told him about the recent events in Jerusalem. They explained how the women who had gone to the tomb found it empty and came back in a state of hysteria, saying Jesus had risen. But the disciples could not accept their conclusion.

Then Jesus began to review the Scriptures with them, explaining how they made it clear that the Messiah must suffer before entering into his glory.

When the two disciples reached Emmaus, they asked the stranger to sup with them. "While he was with them at table, he took bread, said the blessing, broke it, and gave it to them. With that their eyes were opened and they recognized him, but he vanished from their sight." *Luke 24:30-31*

The disciples hurried back to Jerusalem and told the Apostles that Jesus was indeed risen and had revealed himself in the "breaking of the bread."

Recall the first time you received Communion. Review the way you receive it now. *Ask Jesus what you might do to make it a richer experience.*

Day three

"Peace be with you." John 20:19

On Easter night a group of disciples gathered in Jerusalem. They met behind locked doors "for fear of the Jews." Suddenly Jesus stood in their midst and said:

"Peace be with you." When he had said this, he showed them his hands and his side. The disciples rejoiced. . . . Jesus said to them again, "Peace be with you. As the Father has sent me, so I send you." And when he had said this, he breathed on them and said to them, "Receive the holy Spirit. Whose sins you forgive are forgiven them, and whose sins you retain are retained."

Thomas, called Didymus, one of the Twelve, was not with them when Jesus came. So the other disciples said to him, "We have seen the Lord." But he said to them, "Unless I see the mark of the nails in his hands and put my finger into the nailmarks and put my hand into his side, I will not believe." John 20:19-25

Many Bible readers see here the origin of the sacrament of Reconciliation. It is a beautiful Easter gift to those who fled Jesus in Gethsemane. They are forgiven, and they are commissioned to forgive others.

Recall a meaningful reception of the sacrament of Reconciliation. What made it special? *Ask Jesus how you can make this sacrament a richer experience for you.*

_____

_____

_____

_____

_____

_____

Now a week later his disciples were again inside
and Thomas was with them.
Jesus came . . . and stood in their midst. . . .
Then he said to Thomas,
"Put your finger here and see my hands,
and bring your hand and put it into my side,
and do not be unbelieving, but believe."
Thomas answered and said to him,
"My Lord and my God!"
Jesus said to him, "Have you come to believe
because you have seen me?
Blessed are those who have not seen
and have believed."   John 20:26-29

Jesus' final words recall this inscription on the tomb of King George VI of England:

I said to the man
who stood at the gate of the year,
"Give me a light
that I may tread safely into the unknown!"
And he replied: "Go out into the darkness
and put your hand into the hand of God.
That shall be to you better than light
and safer than a known way."
Minnie Louise Haskins

Imagine you are Thomas. Experience what he did, using all five of your senses. *Speak to God about how you feel when you walk in the darkness with your hand in his.*

_____

_____

_____

_____

Day five

"Simon, son of John, do you love me?" John 21:15

A delightful resurrection appearance of Jesus took place one morning when the disciples were rowing to shore after a bad night of fishing. Suddenly a stranger on the beach told them to cast their nets one more time to the right. They did. The net had hardly hit the water when it began filling up with fish. As they struggled to retrieve it, John looked again at the stranger. This time he gasped, "It's the Lord!"

When the disciples reached the beach, they saw that Jesus had prepared a fire. On it lay some freshly cooked fish; off to the side was some bread. They all sat down and ate breakfast.

When they finished, Jesus did something unusual and beautiful. He turned to Peter. Three times Jesus asked him, "Do you love me?" Three times Peter answered, "Yes, Lord!" And three times Jesus responded to Peter, "Feed my sheep!"

Peter's threefold affirmation of love erased from his heart his threefold denial of Jesus. And Jesus' threefold response to Peter commissioned him to be the shepherd of Jesus' followers (John 21).

It was a beautiful sunny morning that Peter and the disciples never forgot as long as they lived.

If Jesus asked you, "Do you love me?" what could you point to as proof that you do? *Speak to Jesus about how you can deepen your love for him.*

_____

_____

_____

_____

_____

Day six

They saw a charcoal fire with fish. . . .
And none of the disciples dared to ask him
"Who are you?"
because they realized it was the Lord. John 21:9, 12

A poet has tried to guess what went on in Peter's mind after he had denied he knew Jesus. He writes:

In Peter's dreams
the cock still crowed.
He returned to Galilee
to throw nets into the sea
and watch them sink
like memories into darkness.
He did not curse the sun
that rolled down his back
or the wind that drove
the fish beyond his nets.
He only waited for the morning
when the shore mist would lift
and from his boat he would see him.
Then after naked and impetuous swim
with the sea running from his eyes
he would find a cook with holes in his hands
and stooped over dawn coals
who would offer him the Kingdom of God
for breakfast.

From "The Resurrection Prayers
of Magdalene, Peter, and Two Youths"
by John Shea, in *The Hour of the Unexpected*

What is the poet's point? *Speak to Jesus about how it applies to your life—right now!*

Day seven

I will pour out a portion of my spirit
in those days,
and they shall prophesy.
And I will work wonders in the heavens above
and signs on the earth below.   Acts 2:18-19

Palestine was ruled by Rome in Jesus' time. In almost every country of the Roman Empire it was possible to deify a man. But there was one place where this was impossible. And that was Palestine.

The Jews were monotheists; that is, they believed in only one God. This is why there was only one temple in Israel. The Jews honored the Roman emperor, but they would have let themselves be destroyed rather than profess that he might be God.

How is it possible, then, to explain the incredible turnabout in Jewish thinking that took place among Jesus' followers after his death? Only if Jesus were God could this unthinkable event have taken place—in of all places Palestine.

Had these unlearned men cunningly devised a fictional message, it would have been reasonable to assume that sooner or later one or more of the eleven would have confessed the subterfuge under the pressure of numerous threats of death. But none did. Their witness never wavered. Rather, they experienced an amazing power that even enabled them to work miracles.
Robert L. Cleath, *Christianity Today*

What convinces you most that Jesus rose from the dead? *Speak to Jesus about what caused the transformation in his followers on the first Easter.*

71

8
RESURRECTION TODAY

How does the resurrection impact you today?

We know
that all things work for good
for those who love God. . . .
If God is for us, who can be against us? . . .
What will separate us from the love of Christ?
Will anguish, or distress, or persecution? . . .
No, in all these things
we conquer overwhelmingly
through him who loved us. . . .
Neither death . . . nor any other creature
will be able to separate us
from the love of God
in Christ Jesus our Lord.   Romans 8:28, 31, 35, 37-39

Movie director Cecil B. DeMille was drifting in a canoe on a lake, reading a book. He glanced from the book momentarily and saw a water beetle crawling up the side of the canoe. When it got halfway up, the beetle stuck the talons of its legs to the wood of the canoe and died. DeMille returned to reading his book.

Three hours later he happened to look down at the beetle again. What he saw amazed him. The beetle had dried up, and its back was starting to crack open. As he watched, something began to emerge from the opening: first a moist head, then wings, then a tail. It was a beautiful dragonfly.

As the dragonfly flew away, DeMille took his finger and nudged the dried-out shell of the beetle. It was like a tomb.

This beautiful death-resurrection example from nature helps us appreciate better what happened on Easter Sunday. The parallel between the two is striking. The beetle died fastened to the wood of the canoe. Jesus died fastened to the wood of the cross. Three hours later the beetle went through an amazing change. Three days later Jesus went through an amazing change. The changed body of the beetle no longer had to crawl about, but could fly. Similarly, the risen body of Jesus had new powers to move about.

The body of Jesus that rose on Easter Sunday was totally different from the body of Jesus that was buried on Good Friday. It was not a resuscitated body, restored to its original life—like Lazarus, the son of the widow of Nain, or the daughter of Jairus.

Rather, it was a body that had taken a quantum leap forward into an infinitely higher life. It was a glorified body. It was totally living and totally life-giving.

This week's meditations focus on the central mystery of Christianity: that the risen Jesus is alive and active in our world. The grace you ask for is this:

Lord, help me realize that you are alive
and at work in people's lives—right now.

Day one

*We were indeed buried with Christ
through baptism into death,
so that, just as Christ was raised from the dead
by the glory of the Father,
we too might live in newness of life.*   Romans 6:4

Darryl Stingley was a wide receiver for the New England Patriots in the 1970s. He was hit in a game with the Oakland Raiders and left paralyzed from the chest down. Today he can use only one hand and gets around in an electric wheelchair.

Darryl insists that in some ways his life is better now. Looking back at his pro football days, he says, "I had tunnel vision. All I wanted was to be the best athlete I could, and a lot of other things were overlooked. Now I've come back to them. This is a rebirth for me. . . . I really have a lot more meaning and purpose to live for now."

Those are incredible words from a young man whose dreams of stardom lie buried in an electric wheelchair. But you hear similar things from others who have suffered similar tragedies. They also talk about a personal "resurrection" to new life. They also testify to the central mystery of our faith: Jesus is risen, alive, and active in people's lives today.

Recall a tragedy or setback that served as a kind of resurrection from the dead to new life for you. *Speak to Jesus about what you learned from it.*

Day two

If then you were raised with Christ,
seek what is above,
where Christ is seated at the right hand of God.
Colossians 3:1

In 1963 Brian Sternberg was the world's pole vault champ and the U.S. trampoline champ. One night, while working out, he came down on the edge of the trampoline and was left totally paralyzed. The tragedy left him a bitter young man. But then faith worked a remarkable transformation in him.

Five years later Brian was carried onto the stage of an auditorium in Colorado by a close friend. His long arms and legs flopped back and forth like those of a rag doll. His body weighed only eighty-seven pounds. Placing him in a chair, his friend propped him up with pillows and put a mike in front of his mouth. Brian spoke softly:

My friends . . . I pray to God that what has happened to me will never happen to one of you. . . . Oh, I pray to God you will never know the pain that I live with daily. It is my hope and my prayer that what has happened to me would never happen to you. Unless, my friends, that's what it takes for you to put God in the center of your life.

Brian Sternberg is a living example of the power of the resurrection at work in people's lives.

Relive Brian's bitterness. Relive his newfound faith. *Speak to Jesus about the message Brian's transformation holds for you.*

Day three

"Where, O death, is your victory?
Where, O death, is your sting?" 1 Corinthians 15:55

Dietrich Bonhoeffer was a Lutheran pastor who was executed by the Nazis in 1945, shortly before Easter.

At about sunrise on the morning of his execution, Bonhoeffer was taken from his cell and the verdict of the court martial was read out to him. He was then returned to his prison cell to make final preparations for his execution. The prison doctor describes what happened next.

I saw Pastor Bonhoeffer . . . kneeling on the floor, praying fervently to his God. I was most deeply moved by the way this lovable man prayed, so devout and so certain that God heard his prayer.

At the place of execution, he . . . climbed the steps to the gallows, brave and composed. His death ensued after a few seconds. In the almost fifty years that I worked as a doctor, I have hardly ever seen a man die so entirely submissive to the will of God.

Ederhard Bethge, *Dietrich Bonhoeffer*

Bonhoeffer's composure and deep faith provide another example of the life and power of the risen Jesus at work in people's lives today.

Imagine you are Bonhoeffer. Experience what he did, using all five of your senses. *Speak to Jesus about the quality of your witness to his risen presence in the world.*

_____

_____

_____

_____

Day four

*With great power the apostles bore witness
to the resurrection of the Lord Jesus.*   Acts 4:33

A young man wrote:

*I'm a very logical, scientific-minded person. I need
proofs for everything. Yet, something has happened to
me here in college that I can't explain rationally,
scientifically, or even psychologically.*

*I've become totally preoccupied with Jesus Christ,
who I somehow feel is working within me. . . . I can't
explain this feeling. It came about mainly these past few
months, when I began reading about the early Christians. I was so amazed and in awe of these people that I
found it impossible to question Jesus or doubt who he
is—the Son of God.*

*In short, I guess I began to believe firmly and
thoughtfully what I was taught ever since a child. I
began to see what the apostles and disciples saw and
loved. Jesus became real. . . .*

*I still have occasional doubts, but there remains
that unexplainable something inside me, even in my
doubts. Call it crazy, psychotic, or whatever. . . . I can't
explain it, nor does it go away, nor did I induce it to
come. It just happened.*   Robert Rybicki

Recall a time when you felt Jesus working within
you, as the young man did. *Speak to Jesus about your
experience of his presence in your life—or the lives of
others—right now.*

_____

_____

_____

_____

_____

Day five

His power working in us
is able to do so much more
than we can ever ask for, or even think of.
Ephesians 3:20 (TEV)

A college girl was flying home to Rhode Island for the Easter holidays. Her school year was nearly over and it had been a disaster. She felt that her life no longer held any meaning. Once home, she got into her car and drove down to the ocean. It was after midnight when she arrived. She writes:

I just sat there in the moonlight watching the waves roll up on the beach. Slowly my disastrous first year passed before my eyes. . . . Then all of a sudden the whole experience fell into place. It was over and past. I could forget about it forever. . . .

The next thing I knew, the sun was coming up. As it did I sensed my feelings starting to peak, just as a wave starts to peak before it breaks. It was as though my mind, heart, and body were drawing strength from the ocean. All my old goals and enthusiasm came rushing back stronger than ever. I rose with the sun, got into my car, and drove home.

After her Easter vacation, the girl returned to college, picked up the broken pieces, and successfully completed the year. In the short span of an Easter vacation she had died and risen to a new life.

Recall a similar experience in your own life. *Speak to Jesus about an area of your life in which you need to rise from the dead.*

Day six

O God . . .
you have rescued me from death. . . .
In the shadow of your wings I take refuge. . . .
Your kindness towers to the heavens,
and your faithfulness to the skies.

Psalm 56:13; 57:1, 11

A high school student in Chicago wrote:

I had just finished my paper route. It was Easter morning and I was walking home.

As I passed St. Gall's church, the sun was coming up. I had no intention of going in for Mass, because I was in the midst of a teenage rejection of the church.

Then it happened! I turned around just as the sun struck the silver cross in front of the church. I couldn't take my eyes off its fiery brightness. I was overcome by a sense of what the apostles must have felt two thousand years ago on this same morning. This feeling moved me deeply.

An unseen force seemed to take hold of me, directing my feet up the steps. I opened the door, went in, and knelt down. For the first time in a long time, I prayed. For the first time I understood what Easter was all about.

Have you ever temporarily rejected Christ's Body, the Church? *Speak to Jesus about this rejection and what caused you to return to the Church.*

80

Day seven

"Behold, I am with you always,
until the end of the age." Matthew 28:20

The resurrection of Jesus holds out an invitation to all of us. It invites us to open our hearts to the presence of the risen Jesus in today's world.

It invites us to let Jesus do for us what he has done for so many before us.

It invites us to love again, after our love has been rejected and we are tempted to hate.

It invites us to hope again, after our hope has been dashed to pieces and we are tempted to despair.

It invites us to believe again, after our belief has been shaken and we are tempted to doubt.

It invites us to pick up the broken pieces and start again, after discouragement has crushed us and we are ready to quit.

The resurrection of Jesus is the good news that Jesus has defeated evil and death, and so will we.

It is the good news that nothing can destroy us anymore—not pain, not sorrow, not rejection, not sin, not even death itself.

It is the good news that Jesus is alive and active in our world, ready to work miracles for us, if we but let him.

Which of the above invitations do you feel the resurrection of Jesus is holding out to you, right now, in a special way? *Speak to Jesus about it.*

9
ASCENSION

Can you say yes to Jesus' invitation?

*"All power in heaven and on earth
has been given to me.
Go, therefore,
and make disciples of all nations,
baptizing them in the name of the Father,
and of the Son, and of the holy Spirit,
teaching them to observe all
that I have commanded you.
And behold, I am with you always,
until the end of the age."* Matthew 28:18-20

Terry Fox was a college student in Canada when he contracted bone cancer and had his right leg amputated. He knew he had only a few years to live and wanted to do something significant with them.

Terry decided to run across Canada from Newfoundland to British Columbia, a distance of five thousand miles. He would ask people to sponsor him and then give the proceeds to cancer research. For eighteen months Terry trained, running on his artificial limb.

Finally, on April 12, 1980, he began his run. He dipped his artificial limb into the Atlantic Ocean and set out across Canada. In his pocket were pledges totaling $1 million.

Four months and three thousand miles into the run, Terry collapsed. The cancer had spread to his lungs. When news about Terry flashed across Canada, money came pouring into the hospital. Before Terry died, a short time later, he saw the total reach $24 million.

There's a sequel to that story. A forty-four-year-old mail carrier, Donald Marrs, lived in Cincinnati. Like Terry, he was a cancer victim. Marrs was so moved by Terry's story that he decided to complete his run for him.

He began below Chicago and three months later reached the Golden Gate Bridge. As he headed across it, a drizzle was falling. When he dipped his hand into the Pacific Ocean, completing Terry's run, a huge rainbow arced across the sky. It was a remarkable end to a remarkable run.

There's a parable for us in that sequel. Jesus Christ established God's kingdom on earth, but he died before he could complete it, just as Terry died before he could complete his run.

You are like Donald Marrs. You are being invited to take up the baton from the hand of Jesus and complete the noble task he began. This is what the ascension is all about. On that day two thousand years ago, Jesus commissioned his followers to complete his work on earth.

This week's meditations focus on the ascension of Jesus into heaven. The grace you ask for is this:

Lord, help me say yes to your invitation
to complete your work on earth.

Day one

As the apostles were looking on,
Jesus was lifted up,
and a cloud took him from their sight.   Acts 1:9

Legend says that when Jesus ascended into heaven, the people in heaven were shocked to see his terrible wounds—signs of how much he had suffered.

"Lord," said Gabriel, "do all the people on earth know how much you suffered for them and how much you love them?" "Oh no," said Jesus, "only a tiny handful in Palestine, but they'll tell the rest."

Gabriel looked confused. He knew how fickle people are. He knew how forgetful they are. He knew how prone to doubt they are. So he turned to Jesus and said, "But, Lord, what if those people begin to doubt you? What if they get so involved in living their own lives that they forget to tell others? Or what if the people they tell forget or have doubts? Don't you have a back-up plan—just in case?"

Jesus answered, "I thought about these things, but I decided against a back-up plan. This is my only plan. I'm counting on my friends."

Twenty centuries later, Jesus still has no other plan. He's counting on his friends not to let him down.

How are you spreading the good news of Jesus' love to others? What more could you do in your situation? *Speak to Jesus about this.*

Day two

*"You will receive power
when the holy Spirit comes upon you,
and you will be my witnesses . . .
to the ends of the earth."*   Acts 1:8

The critical moment in a relay race is the passing of the baton from one runner to another. More races are won or lost at that moment than at any other.

Just before ascending to his Father, Jesus passed the baton of responsibility for the kingdom of God to his followers. He commissioned them to complete his work.

Practically speaking, how do you carry out Jesus' commission? There are as many ways to do this as there are Christians. You can do what a twenty-five-year-old Georgetown graduate did. After getting his degree, he entered a seminary. You can do what Albert Schweitzer did. At the age of thirty he abandoned a music career in Europe to study medicine and become a missionary doctor in Africa. You can do what Mother Angelica did. At the age of fifty she began a religious television studio.

But there's yet another way to carry out Jesus' commission. But it is more difficult and more challenging than the ways just described. It is to become witnesses to God's kingdom in your home, your work place, your school. It is to witness to Jesus wherever you find yourself.

What keeps you from doing what people like the Georgetown graduate or Mother Angelica did? *Speak to Jesus about your witness to him.*

Day three

They went forth and preached everywhere,
while the Lord worked with them
and confirmed the word
through accompanying signs.   Mark 16:20

Ruddell Norris was a conscientious young man. He realized that even the "average" person has the responsibility to spread the Gospel. But he was also a shy young man. He found it hard just to talk to people, much less to discuss his faith with them. Then one day he got an idea.

Ruddell did a lot of reading, and he was aware of the many pamphlets explaining the Christian faith. So he decided to set aside a part of his weekly allowance to buy pamphlets. Ruddell placed his pamphlets in places where he thought people would pick them up and read them. For example, he placed them in hospital waiting rooms and in reception areas.

One day a young woman who was a family friend told his parents how she became a convert and how her husband returned to the Church. "It all began with a pamphlet," she said. "I found it in the hospital waiting room."

The story of Ruddell Norris underscores an important point about proclaiming the Good News: There are many ways to do it. It's up to each individual Christian to find a way that he or she, personally, can do it.

What creative way might you experiment with to spread the Gospel? *Speak to Jesus about it.*

Day four

*"The harvest is abundant
but the laborers are few."* Matthew 9:37

Kate Drexel came from a wealthy Philadelphia family. Although she traveled in Philadelphia's "high" society, her parents taught her that wealth is accompanied by the responsibility to share with the needy.

In riding about the city in the 1880s, Kate saw the tragic plight of black children living in hideous slum conditions. What she saw was reenforced by what she read concerning black children in the South and about Native American children in the West. She became convinced that prejudice, broken promises, and unjust laws were creating a cycle of ignorance and powerlessness for these minority children.

Moved to pity, Kate founded the Sisters of the Blessed Sacrament to work among blacks and Native Americans. By the time Mother Katherine Drexel died at the age of ninety-seven, she had spent nearly $20 million of her own personal fortune to educate and care for poor minority children. The order she founded continues her work a hundred years later.

How are you using your talents to complete the work Jesus began? *Speak to Jesus about how you might put them to better use.*

_____
_____
_____
_____
_____
_____
_____

Day five

*"I . . . chose you and appointed you
to go and bear fruit that will remain."* John 15:16

A traveler came upon a barren hillside in the
French Alps. In the middle of it he saw an old man.
On his back was a sack of acorns, and in his hand
was an iron pipe. The man was punching holes in the
ground with the pipe and planting the acorns in the
holes.

Later the old man told the traveler, "I've planted
over a hundred thousand acorns. Perhaps only a tenth
of them will grow." The old man's wife and son had
died and this was how he was spending his final
years. "I want to do something useful," he said.

Twenty-five years later the traveler returned to
the same hillside. What he saw amazed him. It was
covered with a beautiful forest two miles wide and
five miles long. Birds were singing. Animals were
playing. And wildflowers perfumed the air. The
traveler was astounded at how beautiful the hillside
was—all because an old man cared.

At your baptism and confirmation, you received
a sack of acorns and an iron pipe. If you choose, you
can do something beautiful with them. All it takes is
a little effort and a little faith—the kind the old man
had.

Do you tend to plant more trees in life than you
cut down? *Speak to Jesus about what you are doing with
the "sack of acorns and iron pipe" you received when
you were baptized and confirmed.*

Day six

*"Go into the whole world
and proclaim the gospel to every creature."*
Mark 16:15

Composer Giacomo Puccini wrote a number of famous operas. In 1922 he was suddenly stricken by cancer while working on his last opera, *Turandot,* which many now consider his best. Puccini said to his students, "If I don't finish *Turandot,* I want you to finish it for me." Shortly afterward he died.

Puccini's students studied *Turandot* carefully and completed the opera. In 1926 the world premiere was performed in Milan with Puccini's favorite student, Arturo Toscanini, directing. Everything went beautifully until the opera reached the point where Puccini was forced to put down his pen. Tears ran down Toscanini's face. He stopped the music, put down his baton, turned to the audience, and cried out, "Thus far the Master wrote, but he died."

A vast silence filled the opera house. Then Toscanini picked up the baton again, turned to the audience, smiled through his tears, and cried out, "But the disciples finished his work."

When *Turandot* ended, the audience broken into a thunderous applause.

How prepared are you to help finish the Master's work? How well have you studied and understood it? *Speak to the Master about this.*

Day seven

Then I heard the voice of the Lord saying,
"Whom shall I send? . . ."
"Here I am," I said; "send me!" Isaiah 6:8

Dag Hammarskjold became Secretary-General of the United Nations in 1953. He held the post until 1961, when he was killed in a plane crash.

When they cleaned out his apartment, authorities found his personal journal with a note attached to it, saying that it could be published in case of his death. The journal, called *Markings,* became an overnight best-seller. It took us beyond the cool image of the Secretary-General to the heart and soul of the inner man beneath it. One entry concerns the turning point in his life. It reads:

I don't know Who—or What—put the question. I don't know when it was put. I don't even remember answering. But at some moment I did answer yes to Someone—or Something—and at that hour I was certain existence is meaningful and that, therefore, my life in self-surrender had a goal.

Have you ever consciously surrendered yourself to God, saying, "Lord, show me what you want me to do, and I will do it"? How ready are you to say these words to God, right now? *Speak to God about what gives your life meaning and what its goal is.*

10
PENTECOST

How clearly do you see Christ in his Church?

Christ is the head of the body, the church.
Colossians 1:18

A giant television tower rises above the skyline of East Berlin. Just below the tip of the tower is a revolving restaurant. Communist officials intended it to be a showpiece to the West. But a fluke in design turned it into an embarrassment. Whenever the sun hits the tower a certain way, it turns into a huge shimmering cross. Officials tried to repaint the tower to blot out the cross, but to no avail.

Something like that happened in Jerusalem after Jesus' crucifixion. Officials hoped Jesus' death would blot out the Christian movement. Instead, just the opposite happened. The movement spread so spectacularly that by A.D. 64 it was established in faraway Rome. It became so strong there that the Roman emperor, Nero, made it the target of an all-out persecution.

How did Christianity, in just thirty years, grow from a tiny seed into a towering tree? The answer, of course, lies in what happened after Good Friday. Jesus rose, ascended to his Father, and sent the Holy Spirit upon his followers.

This week's meditations focus on Pentecost, the sending of the Holy Spirit on the followers of Jesus. The grace you ask for is this:

Lord, help me see your Church as it truly is:
the extension of yourself into space and time.

During the week you might wish to read what Scripture says about the Holy Spirit. You may find the following passages especially helpful.

Gifts of the Spirit	Isaiah 11:1–9
Many gifts, one Spirit	1 Corinthians 12:1–11
Fruits of the Spirit	Galatians 5:16–26
Taught by the Spirit	1 Corinthians 2:7–16
Life in the Spirit	Romans 8:1–17

Day one

"I will ask the Father,
and he will give you another Advocate
to be with you always, the Spirit of truth."
John 14:16–17

Ancient Jews saw a parallel between the wind and God. The wind's breathlike touch and its stormlike force spoke to them of God's gentle presence and mighty power. The prophets used the wind as an image of God's Spirit (Ezekiel 37:9-10). So did Jesus (John 3:8). Another image of God that Jews used was fire. This grew out of Moses' experience of God in the burning bush, and the people's experience of God at Mount Sinai (Exodus 19:16-18).

It is against this background that we must read the Holy Spirit's descent upon the disciples in an upper room in Jerusalem.

Suddenly there came from the sky a noise like a strong driving wind, and it filled the entire house in which they were. Then there appeared to them tongues as of fire, which parted and came to rest on each one of them. And they were all filled with the holy Spirit and began to speak in different tongues, as the Spirit enabled them to proclaim. Acts 2:2-4

Imagine you are Peter. Experience what he did as the wind and the fire invaded the room. *Speak to the Holy Spirit about the practical meaning of Pentecost for you, personally.*

_____

_____

_____

_____

_____

"It will come to pass in the last days,"
God says,
"that I will pour out a portion of my spirit
upon all flesh." Acts 2:17

A great crowd gathered outside the upper room, attracted by the sound of the "strong driving wind." Peter went out and spoke to the people. He explained how the Spirit had come down upon the disciples, as Jesus had promised. The people were moved by Peter's words. They asked, "What are we to do?" Peter said to them, "Repent and be baptized, every one of you, in the name of Jesus Christ for the forgiveness of your sins; and you will receive the gift of the holy Spirit." *Acts 2:37-38*

With that, about three thousand people were baptized. Their baptism formed them into a single body, which we now call the Church.

But when we use the word *body,* in speaking of the Church, we mean something infinitely more than a *body of people* sharing a common belief. We mean the *Body of Christ* sharing a common life: the risen life of Christ.

And so Pentecost is rightly called the birthday of the Body of Christ, the Church, which is the visible manifestation and extension of the Risen Christ into space and time.

Imagine you are present in the crowd that first Pentecost. What are your thoughts as you present yourself for baptism in response to Peter's preaching? *Speak to the Holy Spirit about his presence within you.*

Day three

Christ is the head of the body, the church.
Colossians 1:18

Sometimes people say, "I can find Christ in my own way and join myself to him. I don't need the Church for that." When you hear this, you want to cry out, "But there is no Christ apart from the Church. Trying to separate Christ and his Church is like trying to separate your head from your body."

Paul discovered this truth in a dramatic way. One day he was on his way to Damascus to arrest Christians and bring them back in chains to Jerusalem. Suddenly a light flashed around him. Paul "fell to the ground and heard a voice saying to him, 'Saul, Saul, why are you persecuting me?' Paul said, 'Who are you, sir?' The reply came, 'I am Jesus, whom you are persecuting.'" *Acts 9:4-5*

Paul was confused. He wasn't persecuting Jesus. He was only persecuting his followers. Then it hit Paul. Jesus and his followers form a single body. Later he expressed this mystery this way: "As a body is one though it has many parts . . . so also Christ. For in one Spirit we were all baptized into one body. . . . Now you are Christ's body, and individually parts of it."
1 Corinthians 12:12-13, 27

Reflect on this truth and its implications: "Trying to separate Christ and his Church is like trying to separate your head from your body." *Speak to Jesus about how to better your relationship with his Church.*

_____

_____

_____

_____

Day four

"You are the light of the world. . . .
Your light must shine before others."
Matthew 5:14, 16

A teacher asked, "What if an incredible explosion destroyed all life on earth except for the thirty of us in this room? Where would the Church be?" The students thought a minute. Then one of them said, "It would be right here in this room. We would be the Church."

That story makes an important point. The Church is not a *place* where people gather. It is the people who gather. But note what was said! The Church is the people who *gather*. To have Church we must *gather* together.

The Church is like the bread and wine that we use for the Eucharist. Hundreds of grains of wheat and hundreds of grapes had to be *gathered* to make them. Only by gathering do we become the Church of Jesus. Only by gathering do we make the Risen Christ visible in today's world.

This is one of the reasons Jesus said to his followers in the Sermon on the Mount, "You are the light of the world. . . . Your light must shine before others." And on another occasion Jesus said, "Where two or three are gathered together in my name, there am I in the midst of them." *Matthew 18:20*

How active are you in your participation of the Lord's Supper? How could you improve or intensify your participation? *Speak to the Lord about this.*

Day five

You were buried with Christ in baptism,
in which you were also raised with him. . . .
If then you were raised with Christ,
seek what is above. . . .
Put on . . . heartfelt compassion, kindness,
humility, gentleness, and patience. . . .
And let the peace of Christ control your hearts,
the peace into which
you were also called in one body.

Colossians 2:12; 3:1, 12, 15

Charles Schulz, who created the *Peanuts* cartoon, once said, "How can you go to something that you are already a part of? If you are a Christian, you are the 'Church.'" Someone else said, "That's precisely my problem with the Church. How can I believe that the Church is the Body of Christ when I see so many second-rate Christians around?"

To that someone else replied, "You're missing the point. That's like saying, 'I can't believe that Beethoven was a musical genius, because I see so many second-rate musicians wrecking his music.' Beethoven isn't on trial; the musicians are. It's the same way with the Church, the Body of Christ. It's not on trial; its members are."

How critical are you of the ministers and the members of your church? Are your expectations of them realistic? *Speak to Jesus about your own witness as a member of his Body, the Church.*

Day six

We, though many, are one body in Christ
and individually parts of one another.
Since we have gifts that differ
according to the grace given to us,
let us exercise them.   Romans 12:5–6

A senior citizen was taking her usual daily stroll for her arthritis. Suddenly she spotted a five-dollar bill on the sidewalk. She was wondering how she could bend over with her arthritic back when along came a blind man with a cane. Telling him about her discovery and her difficulty, she put the tip of his cane on top of the five-dollar bill. His better back enabled him to follow down the cane with his hand and pick up the bill. The two then shared the money.

A Buffalo, Minnesota, project combines a retirement home with a day-care center. The administrator says, "As hard as we try to keep our residents active and alert, those kids do a better job just doing what kids do. Their life, youth, and energy keep everybody stimulated."

"The youngsters are winners too," he says. Kids look beyond wrinkles and gray hair to the heart. What they're looking for is "a hug, a lap, a kind word, a touch, somebody to read them a story, somebody to smile and share with."

How generously do you share your gifts with others? How able are you to "look beyond wrinkles and gray hair to the heart"? *Speak to Jesus about his remarkable ability to do this.*

Day seven

So then
you are . . . built upon the foundation
of the apostles and prophets,
with Christ Jesus himself as the capstone.
Through him the whole structure
is held together and grows into a temple
sacred in the Lord. Ephesians 2:19-21

Years ago there was a delightful show on television. Although it was aimed at children, a lot of adults enjoyed it too. The show featured a cartoonist who would invite children to take his pen and make a couple of scribbles on a sheet of clean paper.

Then against a background of lively music, the cartoonist would transform the scribbles into a beautiful drawing. One scribble became a girl's ponytail; another became the branch of a tree.

In a sense, that's what God wants to do with us. God wants to take our doubts, our selfishness, our impatience—our flaws—and make something beautiful out of them.

God wants to do more. In Jesus, and with the help of the Holy Spirit, God wants to fashion us into the temple of the divine presence on earth.

Do you believe with your whole heart that God wants to take you—with all your flaws—and make something beautiful out of you? *Speak to God about what this might be.*

_____

_____

_____

_____

_____

11
CONTEMPLATION ON GOD'S LOVE

How clearly do you see God in all things?

"Amen, I say to you,
whoever does not accept the kingdom of God
like a child will not enter it."   Mark 10:15

Some years ago the *Chicago Tribune* carried an article entitled "Taking a Walk with My Grandson," by Amelia Dahl. It was written in dialogue form and went something like this:

Ricky	*Grandma, why do trees take off their clothes in the fall?*
Grandma	*Because they're worn out and must be turned in for new ones.*
Ricky	*Where do they get the new ones?*
Grandma	*From the ground, where Mother Nature is busy preparing a new spring wardrobe for them.*
Ricky	*Grandma, ever notice how the sky looks like an upside-down lake?*
Grandma	*And the little white clouds look like sailboats, don't they?*

Ricky	*I wonder where they're sailing to.*
Grandma	*Maybe to a cloud meeting.*
Ricky	*What would they do there?*
Grandma	*Probably decide if the earth needs more rain.*
Ricky	*Gee, God thinks of everything, doesn't he, Grandma?*

Ricky's grandma is a beautiful example of someone who has kept a childlike wonder. To wonder means to see as children see. It means to see things as if you were looking at them for the first time. It means to see them with the newness they had when they tumbled fresh from the creative hand of a loving God. To wonder is to look at a wheat field after a rain and see in it the footprints of God. It is to look into the eyes of a child and see in them the fingerprints of God.

This week's meditations focus on the visible world around you. The grace you ask for is this:

Lord God, help me see in every created thing
a reflection of yourself and your love.

End each meditation this week with this prayer of Saint Ignatius. It reminds us that love involves mutual giving. Love cannot restrict itself to words, but must overflow into action.

Take, Lord,
and receive all my liberty, my memory,
my understanding, and my entire will—
everything I hold dear.
You have given them to me.
I now place them at your service,
to be used as you wish.
Give me only your love and your grace.
That is enough for me.

During the week you may wish to go for an occasional "prayer walk" by yourself. If you can do this at sunrise or sunset by a lake or in a park, great!

Day one

O LORD, my God, you are great indeed! . . .
You make the clouds your chariot;
you travel on the wings of the wind. . . .
You water the mountains from your palace;
the earth is replete
with the fruit of your works. . . .
In wisdom you have wrought them all.
Psalm 104:1, 3, 13, 24

Arthur Gordon had a remarkable scout master in his boyhood. The leader used to take his troops on hikes, not saying a word to them. After each hike he would challenge the boys to describe what they saw.

Invariably they hadn't seen a fraction of what the scout master had seen. He would wave his arms in vast inclusive circles and shout, "Creation is all around you. But you're keeping it out. . . . Stop wearing your raincoat in the shower!" Gordon says:

I've never forgotten that ludicrous image of a person standing in a shower bath with a raincoat buttoned up to his chin. . . . The best way to discard the raincoat I've found is to expose yourself to new experiences. It's routine that dulls the eyes and deadens the ear. . . . Get rid of that raincoat and let creation in!

In what sense do you wear a raincoat in the shower when it comes to creation? *Speak to Jesus about his love for his Father's creation.*

_____

_____

_____

_____

_____

_____

Be still and know that I am God.
Psalm 46:10 (Grail translation)

One drizzly morning Barry Lopez got up early and went for a walk in the woods. As he walked along under the pines and the cedars, he recalled seeing his grandfather go off through these same woods years before.

As Barry continued to walk in the drizzle, he came to a clearing in the woods. There he knelt down and laid his hands on the damp earth. It gave him a feeling of being united with all of creation.

Barry recalled how his grandfather had told him that if he ever felt lonely, he should go for a walk in the woods, be quiet, and do whatever he felt moved to do—like kneeling down and laying his hands on the damp earth.

Half an hour later Barry started back to the house. He felt renewed. Then he remembered why his grandfather used to go for morning walks in the woods. It was the way he said his morning prayers. He would always end up on the other side of the woods, standing on the beach, with his hands in his pockets, listening to the ocean.

———————

Recall a walk in a woods—or along a city street—that turned your thoughts to God and refreshed your spirit. *Speak to Jesus about his use of the outdoors to pray and to refresh his spirit.*

_____

_____

_____

_____

_____

_____

*"When your eye is sound,
then your whole body is filled with light."*
Luke 11:34

In one of his books, James Carroll recalls how the comic section of the Sunday newspapers used to carry printed games. For example, there would be a picture of a family enjoying a picnic. Beneath the picture was printed the question, "Can you find the man hidden in this scene?" You'd look and look but wouldn't see him. Then you'd turn the paper around to get a different view. Suddenly, in a cloud you'd see an ear. Then, in the leaves of a tree you'd see a mouth, and so on, until you'd see an entire man's face smiling out at you from the page.

Once you saw that man, that picnic scene was never the same again. For you had found the hidden man. You had seen his smiling face.

It's that way in real life. We Christians know, by faith, that there's a person hidden away in every scene of our daily life. And that person is God. And God is not there in a purely passive way. God is there as a giver of gifts: life, talents, air, food, refreshing rain. Everything in our world is a gift of love to you from God.

Why is it hard for you to think of life, talents, air, and food as gifts of love from God? *Ask Jesus, "If you have given me so much, what ought I to give you in return?" and listen for his response.*

_____

_____

_____

_____

Day four

"Sun and moon, bless the Lord. . . .
Stars of heaven, bless the Lord. . . .
All you birds of the air, bless the Lord. . . .
All you beasts, wild and tame, bless the Lord;
praise and exalt him above all forever."

Daniel 3:62–63, 80–81

Saint Francis used to walk about addressing the sun and the moon as "brother" and "sister." Unlike Francis, you and I don't think of the sun and the moon as being a brother or sister. But is it Francis who is odd for doing this? Or is it us for *not* doing so?

Schooled in Western sciences, we are trained to see how different things are from one another. Schooled in a different science, Francis was trained to see how similar things are to each other. He didn't see himself as standing outside nature, but as being a part of it.

For example, Francis was trained to see that the rose came from the loving hand of God. If God was parent to the rose, was not the rose Francis's sister?

Francis called the sun and the moon "brother" and "sister" because they were a part of God's family. They had a bit of God in them, just as he did.

———————

If God's gifts to you contain a bit of God in them, what ought your gifts to God contain? *Speak to God about what gift you could give him in appreciation for his self-gift to you.*

———————————————————
———————————————————
———————————————————
———————————————————
———————————————————

Day five

The heavens declare the glory of God.   Psalm 19:2

I sing the mighty power of God,
That made the mountains rise;
That spread the flowing seas abroad,
And built the lofty skies. . . .

I sing the goodness of the Lord,
That filled the earth with food;
He formed the creatures with his word,
And then pronounced them good.
Lord, how your wonders are displayed,
Where e'er I turn my eye:
If I survey the ground I tread,
Or gaze upon the sky!

There's not a plant or flower below,
But makes your glories known;
And clouds arise, and tempests blow,
By order from your throne;
While all that borrows life from you
Is ever in your care,
And everywhere that man can be,
You, God, are present there.   Isaac Watts (1713)

Reread this hymn slowly and prayerfully, pausing briefly after each stanza to reflect on it. *Speak to God after each reflection.*

Day six

What can I offer the LORD
for all his goodness to me?   Psalm 116:12 (TEV)

The Spiritual Exercises of St. Ignatius end with a classic reflection called "Contemplation on God's Love." The first half proceeds by two stages.

First stage. Reflect on how God created you and lavished on you talents from within and gifts from without: loved ones, a beautiful universe to be your home, membership in the Church, the space-time manifestation of his risen Son.

All these talents and gifts are *signs* of God's love for you.

Second stage. Reflect on how God dwells in every part of the beautiful universe that is your temporary home: stars, giving them existence; plants, giving them life; animals, giving them sensation; loved ones, giving them understanding; yourself, giving you existence, life, sensation, and understanding.

Again, all these gifts, crowned by the self-gift of God's own person, translate into *signs* revealing the height, depth, breadth, and width of God's love for you: You are made in God's image and likeness to be God's own living temple.

Meditate on each stage. Then, with the psalmist, ask yourself, "What can I offer the LORD for all his goodness to me?" *Speak to the Holy Spirit about the possible offerings you might make.*

_____

_____

_____

_____

_____

Day seven

*What can I offer the L*ORD
for all his goodness to me?   Psalm 116:12 (TEV)

Yesterday you pondered the first half of Saint Ignatius' "Contemplation on God's Love." Today you will ponder the second half. It also proceeds by two stages.

First stage. Reflect on how God *toils* for you in all of creation: in heavenly bodies, plants, animals, family, and friends. In other words, God's love extends even to entering into the struggle of life for you—like a mother giving birth to a child, or like a father toiling for his family. This entry into the struggle of life leads to the death of God's own Son on the cross.

These incredible labors are signs pointing to God's infinite love for you.

Second stage. Reflect on how God's gifts descend on you—like rain from above, like rays of sunlight. As the clouds shower moisture on the earth, and as the sun floods it with light and warmth, so God rains down on you his love, his mercy, his goodness.

Again, this rain of gifts is a shower of signs indicating the height, depth, breadth, and width of God's infinite love for you.

Meditate on each stage. Then, with the psalmist, ask yourself, "What can I offer the LORD for all his goodness to me?" *Together with Jesus and the Holy Spirit, present your offering to the Father.*

APPENDIX A

The Spiritual Exercises of St. Ignatius

The goal of *The Spiritual Exercises of St. Ignatius* is to help people find, choose, and live out God's will for them. The Exercises are divided into four parts, called "Weeks":

First Week—invites you to evaluate how well you are living your life according to the purpose for which God created you.

Second Week—shows how Jesus lived his life according to the purpose for which his Father sent him into the world and invites you to imitate and follow Jesus.

Third Week—strengthens and confirms your resolve to imitate and follow Jesus.

Fourth Week—begins your journey with Jesus to a fuller and richer Christian life.

The Spiritual Exercises of St. Ignatius are normally made in a retreat house, where retreatants do them full time for thirty days. Saint Ignatius realized, however, that not everyone could take off thirty days to do this. So, in the 19th Annotation of his Exercises, he explains how the meditations can be done at home over a longer period of time. This meditation program is designed to help you do just that.

A popularized "text" of *The Spiritual Exercises of St. Ignatius* is *Modern Spiritual Exercises: A Contemporary Reading of the Spiritual Exercises of St. Ignatius* by David Fleming, available in Image (Doubleday) paperback.

APPENDIX B

Spiritual guide

The ideal spiritual guide for someone using this book is a spiritual director schooled in *The Spiritual Exercises of St. Ignatius.* If such a person is not available, a priest, minister, nun, brother, or lay person may serve as the spiritual guide.

The guide's role is to help the meditator come to grips with the meditation exercises in this book. The real work is between the meditator and the Holy Spirit. The guide is a kind of spiritual midwife in this important process.

The guide's role is particularly important when it comes to young people: high school or college students. In such cases, the guide also serves as a *guarantor,* in George Herbert Meade's famous use of the word.

Guarantors are "significant others" who guide and affirm young people. They are not father-mother substitutes. They are simply adults who respect young people and are, in turn, respected by them. Guarantors are credible people who have earned a right to be heard. They are persons whom young people trust and feel at ease with.

When it comes to spiritual guidance, a guarantor is the kind of person described in the Japanese *Zenrin:* "If you wish to know the road up the mountain, you must ask someone who goes back and forth on it."

In other words, a spiritual guide is someone who is praying on a daily basis—or is willing to begin such a practice. A guide is one who values meditation enough to want to share it with others. A guide understands that you cannot really teach another person to pray. You can only share how you pray. A guide never forgets the words of Saint Therese of Lisieux:

One must banish one's own tastes and personal ideas and guide the other along the special way Jesus indicates for them, rather than along one's own particular way.

Finally, a guide is one who supports and encourages the meditator. This means being able to discuss the meditator's personal and home life, for these are bound to impact the meditator's ability to pray and come to grips with these exercises.

It goes without saying, therefore, that a guide must be secure enough to be rejected by the meditator and resilient enough to weather the difficult situations all spiritual guides encounter. Insecure people should not guide other people. Success is too important to them. The best guides are often people who are successful in another job in life. This success gives them the security they need to let the Holy Spirit work in the Spirit's own time and own way.

APPENDIX C

Small group meetings

The ideal group size is about eight to ten members, who meet weekly after completing each chapter. Begin each weekly meeting with the following prayer:

Lord Jesus, you said that
wherever two or three gather in your name,
you are there with them.
We are two or three;
we are gathered in your name;
and we believe you are with us.

May all our thoughts and sharing
be guided by the Spirit and directed solely
to the greater honor and glory
of God, our loving Father.

End each meeting with a Scripture reading (see suggested reading for each week). Allow a few minutes of silence following the reading. As the group solidifies in trust, the silence may be followed by a brief shared prayer. Conclude each meeting by having everyone join hands and pray aloud the Lord's Prayer.

The *first meeting* is a get-acquainted session. If group members do not know each other, introductions are in order: name, birthday, birthplace, hobby, special interest, and so on.

Next, members might describe their present prayer practice: when they pray, how often, how long, the form their prayer takes.

Next, members might explain why they decided to become involved in this meditation program and how they hope to benefit from it.

Finally, copies of *Journey* may be distributed. A "sharing guide" for *subsequent meetings* follows. (One question is related to each meditation. Not all questions need to be taken. Nor do the questions have to be taken in the order listed.)

One final point. All *subsequent sessions* should begin with three preliminary questions:

1. What time, place, and posture are you using for your daily meditation? (This question may be dropped after most group members have settled upon a definite time, place, and posture.)
2. Which daily meditation for this week did you find especially fruitful?
3. Would you mind sharing your journal entry for that meditation with the group?

WEEK 1 *Can you face rejection as Jesus did?*
Scripture reading: John 11:45-57

1. How much does fear of ridicule or rejection influence what you do or say in front of others?
2. How do you respond when people put you down or ridicule your ideas?
3. Are you more apt to speak up in praise or criticism of another?
4. What is something that discourages or depresses you right now in your life?
5. Which member of your family do you feel closest to? Least close to? Why?
6. To what extent do you let people's ingratitude for your help cause you to say, "Well, that's the last time I'll ever help anyone!"
7. What thought in the poem by Rudyard Kipling appealed to you most and why?

116

WEEK 2 *Do you understand the Eucharist?*
Scripture reading: Luke 22:14-20

1. Recall an event in your life that gives you joy or strength whenever you recall it.
2. When was the last time you "washed someone's feet" (performed a humble service for another)?
3. What is one thing you would erase from your life if you could?
4. Some people strike their breast, bow, or say a short prayer like "My God and my all" when the priest pauses and holds the Body of Christ after saying "This is my body which will be given up for you." What do you do or say at that moment?
5. What motivates you to continue gathering for the Lord's Supper, when some of your friends have ceased to do this regularly?
6. What song holds special memories for you? Why?
7. What part of the celebration of the Lord's Supper do you find most meaningful to you?

WEEK 3 *How much do you appreciate the Eucharist?*
Scripture reading: Acts 20:7-12

1. What was the most meaningful experience you ever had in relation to the Eucharist?
2. How involved are you in your parish?
3. Some people have set prayers that they say before and after receiving Communion. What do you do at those times?
4. What was the greatest sacrifice you ever made to be present at the Lord's Supper?
5. What keeps you from being a better witness to Christ?
6. If you could make one recommendation to improve the celebration of the Lord's Supper in your parish, what would you recommend?

7. When was the last time you attended Mass voluntarily on a weekday, simply because you felt the desire to do so?

WEEK 4 *Can you say, "Your will be done"?*
Scripture reading: Mark 14:32-42

1. When was the last time you prayed for something and then added, "Not my will, Lord, but your will be done"?
2. When was the last time, apart from the celebration of Mass, that you knelt down to pray? Why did you kneel then?
3. To what extent do you pray for things like finding a parking place, passing a test, or finding something you lost?
4. Why do you think the soldiers "fell to the ground" when Jesus answered "I AM"?
5. Recall a time when you felt God's presence in another person.
6. Recall a time when you were truly frightened.
7. Recall a time when you went into prayer deeply disturbed and came out of prayer deeply composed.

WEEK 5 *Why did Jesus suffer for you?*
Scripture reading: John 19:1-16

1. Recall a mistake you made and had a hard time forgiving yourself for.
2. Why do you think the ancient Jewish Council began with the youngest person present in voting on whether a person was guilty or not?
3. Recall a time when you "followed the crowd" rather than Jesus.
4. What was the worst physical pain you ever suffered? The worst mental pain?
5. What was the cruelest thing you ever did to another person?

6. Where do you see Jesus suffering most in today's world?
7. Do you have a prayerbook? Have you ever composed a poem about Jesus or a prayer to him? Do you carry a prayer or a poem in your wallet?

WEEK 6 *Why did Jesus die for you?*
Scripture reading: Mark 15:33-39

1. Recall a time when you felt totally alone, seemingly abandoned—even by God.
2. What about the "man on the cross" attracts and moves you most?
3. Do you wear a cross or a medal? Does it have an inscription on it?
4. What two evils in today's world would you be willing to suffer a great deal for in order to eradicate them?
5. Do you have a crucifix or a cross in your bedroom? Do you ever use it as an aid to prayer?
6. Recall the first time you learned firsthand that love entails suffering.
7. Recall a time when you went for a walk to think out a problem.

WEEK 7 *What happened Easter morning?*
Scripture reading: John 20:1-10

1. List some ways your life would be different had Jesus not risen from the dead.
2. How do you prepare for the reception of Communion at Mass?
3. When was the last time you received the sacrament of Reconciliation? Why don't you receive it more often?
4. How do you resolve "doubts" or questions about your faith when they arise?

5. If Jesus asked you, "Do you love me?" what are three things you could point to as evidence that you do?
6. What is the point of the poem by John Shea?
7. What convinces you most that Jesus rose from the dead?

WEEK 8 *How does the resurrection impact you today?*
Scripture reading: Romans 8:35-39

1. Recall a time when a setback or tragedy led to a "resurrection" from death to new life for you.
2. What was the most serious injury you ever suffered? How did it affect you spiritually?
3. Have you ever seen anyone die? What effect did it have on you?
4. Have you ever felt Jesus "working" within you?
5. The college girl who went to the beach worked out her problems there. Where do you usually go to work out your problems?
6. Have you ever stopped going to church for a period of time? What made you stop? What brought you back?
7. If Jesus agreed to work any miracle of your choice for you, what would you ask him to do and why?

WEEK 9 *Can you say yes to Jesus' invitation?*
Scripture reading: Acts 1:1-11

1. List some things that a person like yourself can do to spread the good news about Jesus.
2. Have you ever considered committing your life to Jesus after the fashion of the Georgetown graduate or Mother Angelica? Would you be willing to seriously consider such a commitment?

3. If you are a parent, do you make sure your children contribute to the Church? If you are a student, how much do you contribute weekly to the Church and its work?

4. Give one example of how you try to translate your faith into action.

5. Using the imagery in the story of the man who planted acorns, do you tend to cut down more trees than you plant?

6. How prepared are you to make a substantial commitment to finishing the Master's work?

7. How prepared are you to say to God right now, "Show me what you want me to do, and I will do it"?

WEEK 10 *How clearly do you see Christ in his Church?*
Scripture reading: Acts 2:1-13

1. What image comes to mind when you hear the term *Holy Spirit?*

2. What image comes to mind when you hear the word *church?* What image came to mind for Saint Paul?

3. Name one concrete thing you could do to better your relationship with the Church.

4. How active are you in your participation in the Lord's Supper? Do you sing? Respond to the prayers? Serve? Usher? Assist as lector?

5. How critical are you of the ministers and the members of your church? Are you realistic in your expectations of them?

6. How prone are you to judge people by externals, which are frequently misleading?

7. How convinced are you that you have a special role to play in the completion of the work Jesus gave to his Church? How can you decide what it is?

WEEK 11 *How clearly do you see God in all things?*

Scripture reading: 1 John 4:7-16

1. What outdoor activities do you engage in? What is your favorite outdoor place?

2. How often do you take a "prayer walk" or a "prayer jog"?

3. Recall a time when you experienced God's presence, in a special way, outdoors.

4. How easily do you identify with Saint Francis and his appreciation of created nature?

5. What part of the outdoors speaks to you most about God?

6. What answer did you give to the psalmist's question, "What can I offer the LORD for all his goodness to me?"

7. Now that you have completed *The Spiritual Exercises of St. Ignatius,* what are your plans? What are some possibilities that the Holy Spirit has put into your mind to consider?